APR 2 9 1987

HOW
TO ENJOY
OPERA

HOW TO ENJOY OPERA

Charles Osborne

Series Editor Melvyn Bragg

PIATKUS

First published in 1983 by Judy Piatkus (Publishers) Limited of Loughton, Essex
Reprinted 1984

British Library Cataloguing in Publication Data

Osborne, Charles
    How to enjoy opera.—(Melvyn Bragg's arts series)
    1. Opera
    I. Title   II. Series
    782.1   ML1700

    ISBN 0-86188-144-3

Designed by Zena Flax

Typeset by Phoenix Photosetting, Chatham, Kent
Printed and bound by Mackays of Chatham Ltd

The publishers would like to thank the following organisations and individuals for permission to reproduce the photographs in this book.

Frontispiece: Reg Wilson; page 6: Clive Barda; facing page 14: London Weekend Television; facing page 15: Catherine Ashmore; facing page 24: Andrew March; facing page 25: Donald Southern; facing page 38: Glyndebourne Festival Opera; facing page 39: English National Opera; facing page 48: Glyndebourne Festival Opera; facing page 49 (both): The Raymond Mander & Joe Mitchenson Theatre Collection; facing page 68: English National Opera; facing page 69: Reg Wilson; facing page 76 (both): Glyndebourne Festival Opera; facing page 77: Nigel Luckhurst; facing page 82: Landseer Films/Channel Four; facing page 83: Zoë Dominic.

Frontispiece: Shirley Verrett and Placido Domingo in the Royal Opera production of Bizet's *Carmen*.

contents

A scene from the English National Opera production of Verdi's *Rigoletto* at the London Coliseum in 1982. In the final scene the 'Duke' (Dennis O'Neill), disguised as a GI, visits Sparafucile's down-town bar, complete with jukebox. Jonathan Miller's production was set in New York in the 1950s, with the 'Duke' as a mafia leader and Rigoletto as his barman.

introduction

Opera attracts a great many passions and prejudices. There
are those who hate it and consider it to be 'artificial',
'snobbish'; some kind of upper-class plot to exclude the
general public. Those who love it will make the highest
possible claims for it – as indeed Charles Osborne does in this
book: they judge it to be the most sublime of the arts, even
out-soaring Shakespeare. No pains or purse strings, they
would say, should be spared to give it the very best of
everything – costumes, scenery, staging, orchestral and vocal
splendour. The magnificence of the opera, they believe,
deserves and demands all that can be drummed up for it –
from sponsors, angels and the state. The anti-opera party
claims that far too much money is devoted to something which
they would say is attended largely by people who ought to
pay for their expensive tastes at the going rate and not out of a
limited state arts grant. For many, the great opera house is the
enemy of egalitarianism, the obstacle to fair trading in the arts
and the privileged canker on the culture. For some, those
same houses are monuments to a consumate display of all the
talents – musical, dramatic, scenic – all fused in that genius of
an invention called Opera.

Reasons for dislike and resentment are often based on ignorance or frustration. Most people in this country do not have access to a grand opera house; many who have the access, feel they cannot afford to go; many more believe that opera is somehow NOT FOR THEM. Socially, educationally and psychologically they place themselves apart from Opera-Lovers. Nor is envy to be underestimated. The opera is publicly considered to be the resort of the know-nothing rich, much on a par with St. Moritz for the skiing and the Caribbean for that second little winter break. This is not correct. Most people who go to opera work hard, wait long or scheme relentlessly for tickets they make sacrifices to buy; the level of knowledge and appreciation is high, so is the loyalty. But myths are powerful and the fact that there is a mote of truth in the general public's understanding often blinds them to the beamingly obvious: that opera is greatly enjoyed by a whole variety of people and is in no way beyond the grasp of any intelligent enthusiast. This book aims to help and inform that enjoyment.

Television programmes have already been useful here. There is now a tradition in arts programmes of showing a work in progress. This can and does attract viewers who like to watch a process film. It can and does provide insights which are not widely available. In a documentary film on the making of Mozart's *The Marriage of Figaro*, for example, we had Sir Charles Groves explaining in the simplest and most dynamic terms the way in which Mozart constructed his duets. He illustrated the explanation at the piano: the programme further emphasised it by showing the relevant duet being performed. The idea was made both clear and entertaining; and, though simply explained, it was a profound insight. On another vein, the opera's director, Jonathan Miller, talked about its origins and political significance. Odd as it may now seem, *The Marriage of Figaro* – in which servants make fools of their betters – was, at its time, considered by many of those in authority to be at best an impertinent, at worst a subversive, work. This attitude points to an importance given to opera – an importance increased by its popularity – which seems difficult to imagine today. But Verdi, also, at times, was considered an 'artist of revolt'. His operas were regarded as too partial to the new and disruptive ideas of freedom. Television programmes on the making of opera can put all this in context.

What they can do far less well is to show the power of opera. For this you have to go. To be met by live singers, an orchestra, a well-designed and lit set, fine costumes, good direction – all this made harmonious to the power of that dramatic and musical conjection which is opera – is an experience which can be replicated but one for which there is no proper substitute. For the whole idea is that you are to be confronted by those massed forces, this total work of art.

We are back, though, to the difficulties of location, expense, education. It is worth mentioning some of the excellent recordings of operas which give many people a satisfaction similar to that of reading a play by Shakespeare. Indeed, there will be those who claim that they would rather listen on record to a wonderful cast and orchestra than go to the trouble of attending an indifferent performance; just as Charles Lamb made out a case for preferring the reading of Shakespeare over watching a production. Whatever the particular benefits, however, operas, like plays, were written to be performed; they only fully exist as the artist imagined them when they are performed as he intended them to be.

At the present time there seems to me to be a widespread and growing movement concerned to make opera more available, not only on records and on radio and television – where productions as difficult as Wagner's *Ring* and Verdi's *Rigoletto* have been done with surprising effectiveness – but in opera houses and theatres themselves. There is a determination on the part of young composers/producers/singers not to neglect that untapped public which cannot or will not come to the few great opera houses. Small-scale operas are being mounted. Portable operas are being taken around schools and modest-sized theatres.

There is one production – Peter Brook's *Carmen* – which

points the way to a third and possibly most satisfying alternative. For he does *Carmen* not as a glorious, lavish, cast of thousands, spangled production but as a sparse musical melodrama with four singers and an orchestra of seventeen. It is a riveting interpretation sweeping away not only superfluous costliness but the softening and artificiality which it encouraged. *Carmen*, in short, comes over as real drama and the music works dramatically.

This treatment could not be applied to every opera. Nor am I advocating the demolition of the great houses and the abolition of all the grand sights and effects. Brook's *Carmen*, though, does prove, conclusively, that even the most traditional and 'stagey' opera can have a place in a modern stage which is moving, affordable and in proper contact with a modern sensibility.

Charles Osborne, one of the world's leading authorities on Verdi and a gilt-edged opera buff, is an expert in two ways: in his appreciation of the work and in his method of transmitting what he sees as the basic information. It is impossible, in such a book, to paint the atmosphere of a live performance: the particular tensions and pleasures of that must be experienced. I hope they will be, and more richly experienced, after this book has been read.

Melvyn Bragg

27th January, 1983

1

WHAT IS OPERA?

Anyone who enjoys both drama, whether in films, on television or on the stage, and music is a potential opera-lover, for opera is drama conveyed in music. Indeed, opera has something for everyone who enjoys music, the theatre, singing, dancing and the visual arts; it combines elements of them all. There are many different kinds of opera, just as there are different kinds of novels, or plays or films, and no one is expected to like them all. There are spectacular nineteenth-century operas, elegant eighteenth-century ones; there are comedies, dramas, farces and historical romances; there are great operas, good operas, poor operas and excruciatingly boring operas.

The important thing to realise, if you are only just beginning to know about opera, is that it can be highly enjoyable. But, just as you would not be put off novels for life by a particularly boring one, so you must not be put off the rewarding art form of opera merely because you happen to encounter one that does not strike you as interesting.

Forget any lingering prejudice you may have about opera being only an entertainment for the 'élite', whoever they may be. Opera is for all, and when you go to the opera house for the first time – or to the theatre or hall, for operas are performed in all sorts of places nowadays – you will find yourself in the company not of duchesses wearing tiaras but of people like yourself, people from all walks of life, united in the theatre by their search for entertainment. For opera, like all the art forms, is first and foremost entertaining.

Approach your first opera with an open mind, and with open ears. You may not like it, in which case try again with a different one. Make an effort and you will be amply rewarded. After a little experimenting, you will discover which kinds of operas you find the most entertaining. You may decide that you enjoy the comedies of Mozart more than the sagas of Wagner, or the dramatic Verdi more than the romantic Puccini, or you may find that you prefer the down-to-earth melodrama of Mascagni to the poetic melancholy of Tchaikovsky. The more you see, the more your enjoyment will grow and deepen.

If you were to consult a dictionary to find out what the word 'opera' meant, you would discover a number of differing definitions with one element in common: music. An opera is a theatrical work in which the words are sung instead of spoken. However, not all theatrical works in which the words are sung instead of spoken are operas! In some types of opera, the words are occasionally sung and occasionally spoken; in other types, although all the words are sung, the music is sometimes recognisably melodic and tuneful, while at other times the singers appear merely to be chanting at excessive speed. The *Oxford English Dictionary* states, not very helpfully, that opera is 'A dramatic performance in which music forms an essential part, consisting of recitatives, arias and choruses, with orchestral accompaniment and scenery; also, a dramatic or musical composition intended for this, a libretto or score.' The word 'opera' comes, not surprisingly, from an Italian word derived from the Latin *opus* which means work, and the plural *opera* has become the modern Italian word for work, as in 'Let's go to work', 'The works of Byron', and a musical-dramatic work.

However, most people, whether interested in opera or not, know in the broadest sense what it is: a play in which the drama is carried on more through music and song than through speech. In fact, all the feeling and understanding in opera is carried through the sound. Some of the plays or plots are well known, some are weak, unreal or even absurd, but when combined with glorious music, sublime singing, spectacular costumes and scenery, the result is great theatre – and a very pleasurable and emotionally uplifting experience.

Words are concrete, used to express concrete thoughts and feelings and to deliver practical information; music is, by its very nature, abstract. When the two are put together, the resulting tension creates an excitement and an extra dimension which is denied to the spoken theatre. For example, Shakespeare's *Othello* is a great play, and Verdi's *Otello* which is based on it is a great opera. I think that, if one had seen Shakespeare's *Othello* seventy times one would be hard put to it to derive much enjoyment from a seventy-first encounter. But after seventy performances of the opera one can still find new beauties and subtleties to marvel at. Similarly, Beaumarchais' play *Le mariage de Figaro*, entertaining though it is, is not something one would want to see once or twice a year throughout one's lifetime. But ask any opera-lover whether he is tired of Mozart's opera based on the play and you will learn that he is not, for its riches are inexhaustible. Music brings a greater complexity to the spoken drama and turns it into a different kind of experience.

Many people who have never been to an opera think that they would not like it if they did, and accuse it of being unreal. After all, in real life people do not sing at each other like that. Well, no they do not, but that argument never stopped Fred Astaire and Ginger Rogers, or Mickey Rooney and Judy Garland, or John Travolta and Olivia Newton-John from singing (and dancing) at and with each other. One could, with equal justification, say that people do not speak to each other in blank verse, but I have never heard that point used as an argument against the plays of Shakespeare. Likewise, the fact that people are not usually found stuck to canvas in a frame does not prevent us from appreciating the human form in paintings.

None of the art forms – music, painting, drama or poetry – is an attempt to imitate life but an attempt to comment on it, to describe it, to explain it. Music is used to underline and increase the expressive power of speech in art forms other than opera: in films, for instance, where the drama or the comedy of a scene is often highlighted by the use of 'background' music.

If you feel that opera is unreal, it is important to find something to relate to which has popular appeal and also certain parallels with opera. Musicals such as *West Side Story* or *Jesus Christ Superstar* and operettas such as *The Merry Widow* are full of characters who sing and dance. And just think of Judy Garland in *The Wizard of Oz*, John Travolta in *Saturday Night Fever*, and Julie Andrews in *The Sound of Music*, all of whom burst into song and dance when spoken words alone do not seem adequate to the situation.

It may seem a long step from John Travolta to Enrico Caruso, or from Judy Garland to Joan Sutherland, but once you take that first step along the yellow brick road of song and dance you are setting out towards the land of opera, whether or not you ever get there!

Many musicals certainly come within my definition of opera, musicals having reached a high peak of achievement in the United States. Immigrant European composers led the way – composers like Kurt Weill, whose Broadway shows (among them *Street Scene* and *Lost in the Stars*) are the forerunners of those of Richard Rodgers (*Oklahoma!*), Lerner and Loewe (*My Fair Lady*), Leonard Bernstein (*Candide, West Side Story*) and Stephen Sondheim (*Sweeney Todd*). If you have enjoyed any of these shows, you are certainly not someone who is implacably opposed to the idea of opera. Even the rock musicals of Andrew Lloyd Webber (*Jesus Christ Superstar, Evita*) have been described as operas, and the description is not at all far-fetched.

But is not operatic music a completely different kind of music from that of the pop song or the musical comedy number? The answer is that it can be, but it does not have to be. Admittedly, Mozart's operas *The Magic Flute* and *The Marriage of Figaro* do not sound very similar to the Beatles, but it is hardly fair to compare eighteenth-century opera with twentieth-century pop. Mozart's operas are not so far removed from the popular music of their own time, the 1780s. People

Sheila Hancock and Denis Quilley in *Sweeney Todd*, Stephen
Sondheim's highly enjoyable modern opera.

danced to their tunes, and turned their arias into popular songs. In the nineteenth century, the songs sung by the fishermen of Naples had much in common with the arias and ensembles in the operas of Rossini and Donizetti, while some of Verdi's tunes reached the repertoire of the street musician almost before they had been heard in the opera house. It may be that the real operas of today are the musicals, which now have widened their scope to embrace drama and tragedy, and can no longer be classified as 'musical comedy'.

For many people opera is the most satisfactory and rewarding of all art forms, but is it not, for all that, still an entertainment for the minority? Of course it is, but so are many other forms of entertainment. It was Oscar Wilde who said that only the auctioneer has to appreciate all forms and styles of art! I think that this is a point worth remembering in an age when we appear to think that, if one is given the right kind of education, one will respond to all art forms. My view is that we are all limited by our own individual temperaments much more than by any educational deficiencies. We should certainly try to extend our range of interests as far as possible, but if I happen to have a temperamental disaffinity with folk-song or Gregorian Chant or minimalist painting, no educator is going to persuade me into an appreciation of them. Some people, when exposed to opera, discover that they like it or that they like certain types of opera. Some people, when exposed to football, discover that they like it. Some people like both opera and football, some dislike them both – and why not?

Of course, once you do discover that you can enjoy opera, it is true that your enjoyment will be enhanced by greater knowledge of it. The more you learn about opera, the more you enjoy it and the more you want to learn about it. And you will go on learning about it for the rest of your life.

Opposite: Richard van Allan as Mustapha in the English National Opera production of Rossini's *The Italian Girl in Algiers*.
This comic opera, full of bubbling wit and tunefulness, made Rossini famous and is still very popular today.

2

THE ESSENTIAL ELEMENTS OF OPERA

composer and librettist

Let me be quite unequivocal about this: operas are made of words and music. The words are certainly important, but the music is more important. An opera can survive a poor libretto if the drama is contained in the music. But if the music is poor, unmemorable or undramatic, not even the most superb libretto can save the opera. I can point to dozens of operas which are not only enjoyable but legitimate works of music drama, whose libretti are seriously flawed – among them Verdi's *Simon Boccanegra*, Weber's *Der Freischütz*, Puccini's *Manon Lescaut* and most of the operas of Meyerbeer – but neither I, nor anyone else, can think of an opera which has survived on the basis of its words if its music is dull, excruciating or dramatically irrelevant.

The relationship of the composer to his librettist is clearly of great importance, and it is not surprising that the greatest opera composers – and those generally agreed to be the top five are Mozart, Verdi, Wagner, Puccini and Richard Strauss – have usually wanted to set up a working partnership of some kind with the right librettist, once he has been found. Mozart's finest operas were written with the literary collaboration of Lorenzo da Ponte; Verdi had two or three librettists whom he enjoyed working with, producing nine operas with Francesco Maria Piave and his two great Shakespeare operas with Arrigo Boito; Puccini used the team of Giuseppe Giacosa and Luigi Illica for his most successful works; and Strauss found his ideal partner in Hugo von Hofmannsthal. Richard Wagner preferred working with Richard Wagner.

composer and librettist

The libretto (or 'the book', as they call it in the Broadway musical world) may be an original piece by the librettist or, more frequently, be his adaptation of an existing work, usually a play, sometimes a novel. One of Da Ponte's three libretti for Mozart was an adaptation of a popular play (*Le Nozze di Figaro*; based on Beaumarchais' *Le Mariage de Figaro*), one was an original work of Da Ponte's own devising (*Così fan tutte*), and one was cribbed from the libretto of another opera (*Don Giovanni*).

I shall take Verdi as an example. He ranged over the whole of European drama in search of subjects for his operas. Let us look at what he found.

opera	librettist	original source of libretto
Oberto	Piazza and Solera	unknown
Un Giorno di regno	Romani	play: *Le Faux Stanislas* by Alexandre Pineu-Duval
Nabucco	Solera	play: *Nabucodonosor* by Anicet-Bourgeois and Francis Cornue
I Lombardi (*later* adapted and translated into French as *Jérusalem)*	Solera	poem: *I Lombardi alla prima Crociata* by Tommaso Grossi
Ernani	Piave	play: *Hernani* by Victor Hugo

opera	librettist	original source of libretto
I due Foscari	Piave	play: *The Two Foscari* by Lord Byron
Giovanna d'Arco	Solera	play: *Die Jungfrau von Orleans* by Schiller
Alzira	Cammarano	play: *Alzire* by Voltaire
Attila	Solera	play: *Attila, König der Hunnen* by Zacharias Werner
Macbeth	Piave	play: *Macbeth* by Shakespeare
I Masnadieri	Maffei	play: *Die Räuber* by Schiller
Il Corsaro	Piave	poem: *The Corsair* by Lord Byron
La Battaglia di Legnano	Cammarano	play: *La Bataille de Toulouse* by Joseph Méry
Luisa Miller	Cammarano	play: *Kabale und Liebe* by Schiller
Stiffelio (*later* revised as *Aroldo)*	Piave	play: *Le Pasteur* by Emile Souvestre and Eugène Bourgeois
Rigoletto	Piave	play: *Le Roi s'amuse* by Victor Hugo
Il Trovatore	Cammarano	play: *El Trovador* by Antonio García Gutiérrez
La Traviata	Piave	play: *La Dame aux camélias* by Alexandre Dumas *fils*
Les Vêpres siciliennes	Scribe and Duveyrier	libretto: *Le Duc d'Albe* originally written by Scribe and Duveyrier for Donizetti

opera	librettist	original source of libretto
Simon Boccanegra	Piave (revised by Boito)	play: *Simon Boccanegra* by Antonio García Gutiérrez
Un Ballo in maschera	Somma	libretto: *Gustave III* by Scribe, written for Auber
La Forza del destino	Piave	play: *Don Alvaro, o La Fuerza del sino* by Angel de Saavedra, Duke of Rivas (with one scene from the play, *Wallensteins Lager* by Schiller)
Don Carlos	Méry and Du Locle	play: *Don Carlos* by Schiller
Aida	Du Locle, translated by Ghislanzoni	synopsis by Auguste Mariette
Otello	Boito	play: *Othello* by Shakespeare
Falstaff	Boito	play: *The Merry Wives of Windsor* by Shakespeare

Since words take much longer to sing than to speak, it is obvious that most plays have to be abridged when they are turned into opera libretti. Verdi liked, as far as possible, to undertake this task personally, indicating to his librettist the shape of the libretto and asking him merely to turn the words into Italian verse, which Verdi then set to music. The following letter, written to Cammarano who was his librettist for *Il Trovatore,* reveals how closely Verdi supervised the writing of his libretti:

> Dear Cammarano,
>
> I have read your synopsis and, as a man of talent and very superior character, you will not be offended if I, in my most niggardly fashion, take the liberty of saying to you that, if we cannot retain for this opera all

the novelty and bizarre quality of the Spanish drama, it would be better to abandon it.

It seems to me that, unless I am mistaken, several of the situations lack their former force and originality, and, above all, that Azucena no longer has her strange and novel character. It seems to me that this woman's two great passions, filial love and maternal love, are no longer present in all their power. For example, I would not like to have the troubador wounded in the duel. This poor troubador has so little individuality that, if we take away his valour, what remains to him? How could he interest Leonora, a well-bred lady? And I wouldn't like Azucena to address her narrative to the gypsies nor, in the third act ensemble, to say 'Tuo figlio fu arso vivo etc. etc . . . ma io non v'era etc. etc.' (Your son was burned alive . . . but I was not there), and finally I don't want her to be mad at the end. I should like you to leave her big aria in!! Leonora has no part in the Miserere and the troubador's song, and this seems to me one of the best places for an aria. If you are afraid of giving Leonora too big a role, leave out the cavatina. To express my thoughts better, let me expand into more detail about how I feel this subject should be treated . . .

Verdi then sets out in detail how he wishes the four acts of the opera to be organised, and ends his letter:

I beg you to forgive my rash words. I am no doubt wrong, but I could not refrain from at least telling you how I feel about it. Besides, my first suspicion that you didn't like this play is probably true. If this is so, we still have time to change our minds rather than work on something you don't like. I already have another subject, simple but affecting, which can be said to be almost ready. If you like, I'll send it to you, and we'll think no more of *Trovatore*.
Let me have a word from you about this. And, if you have another subject, tell me of it. Farewell, farewell, my dear Cammarano. Write to me immediately, and believe me yours affectionately for life.

Verdi knew what tone to adopt with each of his librettists. He goaded an excellent libretto out of Cammarano, and composed, in *Il Trovatore,* one of his most popular and most tuneful operas. Incidentally, the 'other subject' which Verdi mentioned in his penultimate paragraph was the Dumas play *The Lady of the Camelias.* This became his next opera, *La Traviata.*

The letter to Cammarano makes clear that the original play (in this case, *El Trovador* by Gutiérrez) was likely to be subject not only to abridgement in the process of being turned into an opera but also to great change.

After enjoying a performance of an opera based on a play, it is often interesting and instructive to see or to read the original. There will usually be differences of emphasis, and often important differences in characterisation or plot. Try reading Sir Walter Scott's *The Bride of Lammermoor* after seeing Donizetti's *Lucia di Lammermoor,* or Murger's novel *The Bohemians* after seeing Puccini's *La Bohème,* or attend a performance of Shakespeare's *Othello* before or after seeing Verdi's *Otello.* Compare Shakespeare's *A Midsummer Night's Dream* with Britten's, or Britten's *Death in Venice* with the Thomas Mann story of that name which inspired Britten to write his opera.

the singers

As anyone who has ever sung in a choir will know, there are four main categories of voice: soprano, contralto, tenor and bass. In other words, high and low male and female voices. There are also voices which do not fit exactly into the ranges generally thought appropriate for them. Mezzo-sopranos, for example, have voices which lie in range and type between soprano and contralto.

The soprano voice has a compass of about two octaves above middle C, coloratura sopranos sometimes having two or three tones above high C. The contralto voice ranges from A below middle C to the A two octaves higher, and the mezzo-soprano range is, as the name implies, halfway between contralto and soprano. The tenor voice usually has a compass of two octaves from around C in the bass clef, while the bass ranges over one and a half octaves or more from the F just

the singers below the bass stave. The baritone is about a tone higher, from G to G.

There are various types of soprano, contralto and so on – high and agile sopranos, small lyrical voices, huge dramatic voices, dramatic tenors who tend to have a heavy, baritonal quality in their middle notes, basses who specialise in noble, grave roles, and those whose voices render them more suitable for comic parts. The buffo bass or comical bass is a properly recognised category, but I have yet to hear of anyone admitting to be a comical soprano!

The higher voices, soprano and tenor, have come to be thought most appropriate for romantic roles, while the villains or the friends of hero and heroine tend to be sung by the contraltos (or nowadays by the mezzo-sopranos, for there seem to be fewer real contralto voices about), baritones and basses. It was not always so, and indeed the modern baritone voice really only came to be recognised at the beginning of the nineteenth century. In Mozart's operas, the musical notes of some roles tell us they should be sung by voices of baritone range but in fact they were designated bass. With the exception of Don Ottavio (tenor), the ineffectual fiancé of Donna Elvira, all the male roles in Mozart's *Don Giovanni* were written for voices which Mozart thought of as bass. However, there is a clear distinction between the heroic baritone of Giovanni himself, the comic bass of Leporello, the lyrical bass or *basso cantante* of Donna Anna's father, and the lyrical baritone of Masetto. Even as early as Mozart's day, the evil characters were not always those with the deepest voices. In *The Magic Flute,* for example, it is the Queen of Night with her glittering coloratura and extraordinarily high soprano who personifies evil, and the bass Sarastro who radiates humanity and warmth.

Whether villainous or heroic, or simply complex human beings who are capable of being either, there are many leading characters in opera whose voices are not those of the romantic soprano or tenor. Examples are to be found in the title-roles in *Boris Godunov* (bass), *Billy Budd* (baritone), *Wozzeck* (baritone), *Falstaff* (baritone), *Nabucco* (baritone), *The Barber of Seville* (baritone), *Eugene Onegin* (baritone), *Cenerentola* (mezzo-soprano), *The Italian Girl in Algiers* (mezzo-soprano).

Just as, in the spoken theatre, certain roles become

associated with great interpreters – for example Kean's Othello, Irving's Thomas à Becket, Gielgud's Hamlet, Olivier's Richard III, Edith Evans's Lady Bracknell, Edwige Feuillère's Marguerite Gautier – so do operatic roles tend to find their great interpreters. These singers come almost to 'own' the roles for the length of time that they are capable of performing them (and sometimes for years after they have ceased being capable of performing them!). Older opera-goers can still remember with awe Rosa Ponselle as Norma in Bellini's opera of that name, the great Russian bass Chaliapin as Boris Godunov, Caruso as Canio in *Pagliacci*, Lotte Lehmann as the Marschallin in *Der Rosenkavalier*, Richard Tauber breathing life and warmth into the staid character of Don Ottavio in *Don Giovanni*, Gigli as Rodolfo in *La Bohème*. (Most of these singers left gramophone recordings of their performances in their great roles.)

The middle-aged opera-lover will have his own more recent list of great interpretations, exciting and definitive performances which he has experienced in the opera house. My own personal list would include Marjorie Lawrence as Amneris in *Aida*, Irmgard Seefried as Susanna in *The Marriage of Figaro*, Leontyne Price as Aida, Elisabeth Schwarzkopf and Christa Ludwig as Fiordiligi and Dorabella in *Così fan tutte*, Julius Patzak in *Tales of Hoffman*, Jussi Björling in *La Bohème*, Zinka Milanov in *Il Trovatore*, Lisa Della Casa and Dietrich Fischer-Dieskau in *Arabella*, Tito Gobbi in almost everything he did, especially Falstaff, Iago, Scarpia in *Tosca* and Don Giovanni, Erich Kunz as Papageno in *The Magic Flute*, Nicolai Gedda as Nemorino in *L'Elisir d'amore*, Gustave in *Un ballo in maschera*, Benvenuto Cellini in Berlioz's opera, Orpheus in Gluck's *Orpheus and Euridice*, and Hoffmann in *Tales of Hoffmann*, Joan Sutherland in *Lucia di Lammermoor, I Puritani, La Fille du régiment, La Traviata* and *Lucrezia Borgia*, Giulietta Simionato as Azucena in *Il Trovatore* and Amneris in *Aida*, Leyla Gencer as Lady Macbeth, Donizetti's Anna Bolena and Rossini's Elizabeth I, Sena Jurinac as the Composer in *Ariadne auf Naxos*, Peter Pears as Peter Grimes, Joan Hammond as Aida, Carlo Bergonzi in *La Forza del destino, Pagliacci* and *Tosca*. I stop, not because I have run out of names but because I realize I could continue for several pages.

the singers   Today's younger opera-goers are equally fortunate in the splendid array of singers now in their thirties and forties such as Hildegarde Behrens, Ileana Cotrubas, Kiri Te Kanawa, Valerie Masterson, Grace Bumbry, Montserrat Caballé, Placido Domingo, José Carreras, Sherrill Milnes, Giacomo Aragall, Shirley Verrett, Carol Neblett, Rita Hunter, Agnes Baltsa, Renata Scotto, Mirella Freni, Ruggero Raimondi, Lucia Popp and many others.

Among some of the most famous performances by international singers of the 1980s are the following, which you ought to catch if you can. Most of these singers appear in leading opera houses in Europe and north America, and are frequently to be heard at the Royal Opera House, Covent Garden, London: Jon Vickers as Peter Grimes in Benjamin Britten's opera *Peter Grimes*; Grace Bumbry as Salome in Strauss's *Salome* and as Lady Macbeth in Verdi's *Macbeth*; Katia Ricciarelli as Verdi's *Luisa Miller*; Nicolai Ghiaurov as Mussorgsky's *Boris Godunov*; Nicolai Gedda as Hoffmann in Offenbach's *Tales of Hoffmann* or Lensky in Tchaikovsky's *Eugene Onegin*; Teresa Berganza as Angelina in Rossini's *La Cenerentola* or as Rosina in the same composer's *The Barber of Seville*; Hermann Prey in the title-role of *The Barber of Seville*; Agnes Baltsa as Amneris in Verdi's *Aida*, Christa Ludwig as the Marschallin in Strauss's *Der Rosenkavalier*; Teresa Stratas as Lulu in Alban Berg's *Lulu*, Walter Berry as the same composer's Wozzeck, Valerie Masterson in the tile-role in Massenet's *Manon* or Marguerite in Gounod's *Faust*; Lucia Popp as Pamina in Mozart's *The Magic Flute*; Pauline Tinsley as Abigaille in Verdi's *Nabucco* or the Dyer's Wife in Strauss's *Die Frau ohne Schatten* (The Woman without a Shadow); Joan Sutherland as Lucy Ashton in Donizetti's *Lucia di Lammermoor* or singing the title-role in *Lucrezia Borgia*; Edita Gruberova as Zerbinetta in Strauss's *Ariadne auf Naxos*; Rita Hunter as Brünnhilde in Wagner's *Die Walküre* or *Götterdämmerung*; Kiri Te Kanawa as the Countess in Mozart's *The Marriage of Figaro*.

The role of the chorus is much more important in some operas than in others. The chorus is required only when the action involves a large number of characters, or when scenes take place in a public place where a crowd is gathered

Valerie Masterson as Manon, one of her greatest roles,
with John Brecknock as Des Grieux, in the English National
Opera production of Massenet's *Manon*.

A spectacular scene from Verdi's *Aida* at the London Coliseum.

together. In some modern operas it is dispensed with entirely, **the singers**
though composers of the eighteenth and nineteenth centuries
made great use of the chorus to comment on events and to
participate in the final scenes, adding a great mass of choral
sound to the climaxes. Rossini, Donizetti and, in his early
operas, Verdi tended to begin with choruses of citizens or soldiers or whatever, who dispersed when the principal singers
entered. But in the later operas of Verdi, and those of Puccini,
the chorus is used more rationally, and only when the dramatic situation calls for it. *Aida,* for example, begins with two
men conversing. It is in the second scene of Act II, when the
populace turns out to welcome the returning warriors, that
Verdi makes spectacular use of the chorus. And in *La Bohème*
Puccini needs a chorus only in Act II, to enact the populace of
Montparnasse as they stroll through the streets. Benjamin
Britten's *Peter Grimes* has a chorus who represent the villagers, and his *Billy Budd* has only a male chorus, who are the
crew of the *Indomitable,* while some of his operas, among
them *The Turn of the Screw* and *Death in Venice,* do not
require a chorus at all.

the conductor

The role of the conductor in opera is of the greatest importance. In the staging of an opera, he and the director are jointly
responsible for the interpretation of the composer's work. It is
essential, therefore, that conductor and stage director should
agree on their approach to the opera they are staging. The
director's work with the company begins with the first rehearsal, but the conductor is involved, or should be, even earlier
than this. He and the director will have cast the leading roles,
but the conductor will usually want to discuss interpretation
with the singers while they are still learning their roles.

In performance, it is the conductor's task to co-
ordinate what is going on in the orchestra pit with what is happening on the stage. At the same time, he is responsible for
the musical performances of the orchestra, the chorus and the
solo singers. The opera conductor has a more complex task
than the conductor in a concert hall, for he must be not only a

the conductor competent musician but also a man of the theatre, with a knowledge of theatre practice, and an instinct for theatrical timing as well as that instinct for musical timing which one calls a sense of rhythm. In the preparation of the opera, he and the director will have had an equal share of the responsibility. But when the house lights are lowered, and the conductor enters the orchestra pit and raises his baton to begin the performance, the success or failure of that performance is very largely in his hands. An individual singer may not be at his best, or something may go wrong with the lighting, but if the conductor can maintain and convey his sense of the drama, and sustain it from scene to scene, from act to act, to the conclusion of the opera, the audience will leave with a feeling of satisfaction.

There are some first-rate symphonic conductors who have absolutely no sense of the theatre, and the more sensible of them do not attempt to conduct opera. However, some of the greatest conductors of opera today are men who are equally at home in the concert hall: Carlo Maria Giulini, Herbert von Karajan, Claudio Abbado, Riccardo Muti, Carlos Kleiber, Leonard Bernstein, Georg Solti. Just as a singer will be better in some roles than in others, so conductors will excel in the work of some composers and not in others. Karajan is superb in Strauss and Verdi; Solti is more successful in extrovert pieces than in, for example, *Parsifal.* Few can conduct finer performances of the *bel canto* operas than Richard Bonynge, but he is not likely to be found conducting Bruckner in the concert hall.

The conductor must not only judge the right tempo for each aria, and each scene in the opera, he must also be flexible enough to adjust to suit the situation of the moment: this singer will have a tendency to linger, that one finds it difficult to produce enough volume at the climax of his aria and must be helped, instead of being hindered by a too-loud accompaniment. A famous singer once said that, for Verdi's *Il Trovatore,* which is very much a singers' opera, all you need are the four greatest singers in the world. It is not true: you can get by with singers of lesser attainment. But even if you do have the four greatest singers in the world, if the conductor is inadequate you will not have a very enjoyable performance.

the director

The director or producer is the man who actually stages the opera, rehearses the singers in their movements, discusses their roles with them and co-ordinates their interpretations, and has an over-all view of the opera and its performance. He is as comparatively recent an innovation in opera as he is in the theatre. In the eighteenth and nineteenth centuries, the craft of the director was hardly recognised at all. One of the actors, often the leading player, made sure that the performers did not actually bump into one another as they walked about the stage, and that was all. In nineteenth-century productions of opera, there were stage managers who took on this function, but it was not until composers such as Verdi and Wagner began to insist on being present at rehearsals to supervise the staging that the concept of 'production' emerged. Wagner's *Ring* and *Parsifal* were 'produced' at Bayreuth by the composer, and the later operas of Verdi were certainly 'produced' by the composer at La Scala, Milan. But it is with the conductor-composer Gustav Mahler, who was in charge at the Vienna Opera from 1897 to 1907, that modern ideas of production took hold. Mahler was responsible not only for the musical preparation of the operas he staged, but also for their staging. His productions of the operas of Mozart laid the basis for a style which can still be discerned in contemporary productions of Mozart in Vienna.

During the twentieth century, the role of the director came to assume an ever-increasing importance. Opera can be said to have passed through an era in which the singer held sway, to an age of the conductor, and then to that of the director, which is now just ending. When Melba and Caruso sang in *La Bohème* in the pre-First World War years, it was they whom the audiences came to see and hear. It hardly mattered who was conducting the opera, and it certainly did not matter who had rehearsed the singers from the point of view of the drama. Usually no one had. During the inter-war years the conductor became the star. People went to La Scala to hear Toscanini's Verdi, to Bayreuth for Fürtwangler's Wagner and to Salzburg for Bruno Walter's Mozart and Strauss. In the years since the Second World War, however, we have become

the director   used to hearing about Felsenstein's *Carmen,* Visconti's *Don Carlos,* Zeffirelli's *Lucia di Lammermoor,* Friedrich's *Ring,* Wieland Wagner's *Lohengrin,* Peter Hall's *Don Giovanni,* Rudolf Hartmann's *Rosenkavalier* and so on. Many directors, though not many of the leading directors listed above, have abused their powers by wilfully distorting the operas they have been called on to stage. The present indications are that a quiet but determined revolt of singers, musicians and audiences has been gathering momentum, and that the wilder excesses of opera directors will soon be a thing of the past.

In general, singers, conductor and director are of equal importance in the performance of opera, though there will always be particular operas in which the star singer or the conductor (though, surely, never the director) will take precedence.

design

Stage design in opera does not basically differ from design in the spoken theatre except that, in the international opera houses, it offers more opportunities for lavish sets and costumes than are afforded by most modern plays. Do not let this show of opulence lead you to think that opera productions have to be lavish to be enjoyable. Smaller companies who cannot afford expensive sets or costumes can stage operas, just as small repertory companies can adapt West End plays to their own resources. However, opera productions often remain in the repertory for many years and the sets and costumes are put to good use.

choreography

Choreography is an important element in opera, because ballet was an integral part of the earliest operas, especially in France, and remained essential to French *grand opéra* in the nineteenth century. Plots of the operas had to be manipulated to allow for the inclusion of a ballet, and foreign composers writing operas for Paris were required to provide ballet music for the appropriate scene. Gradually, however, this custom fell **choreography** into disrepute, and ballet or dance subsequently found its way into opera only when called for by the dramatic situation. Nowadays, when these nineteenth-century operas are revived, the ballet is usually omitted.

the economics of opera

No one will be surprised to hear that opera is an expensive business. To the usual expense of staging a non-musical play must be added the cost of an orchestra, a chorus and a conductor. Also, leading singers command much larger fees than leading actors. There are valid reasons for this. First, the singer's career is shorter; an actor can go on playing roles for which he is physically suited for as long as he is capable of walking and talking, but a singer is often past his peak at fifty, though he may go on singing for another ten years. Second, the singer of operatic roles cannot perform every night of the week, as the actor does. If he were to do so, his voice would certainly not last until middle age. A leading singer must plan his appearances and ration them. The tenor Nicolai Gedda tries not to give more than fifty performances a year; the baritone Sherrill Milnes limits himself to sixty-five. A soloist is paid per performance and, if he or she is one of a handful of international stars, is paid in thousands rather than in hundreds of pounds.

Since it would be too difficult for managements to assemble a new orchestra and chorus every time they wanted to stage an opera, it has become the custom for opera companies to be set up in a few large towns. Companies occupy a theatre for a specified number of weeks or months each year, with their own orchestra, chorus, stagehands and nucleus of singers, to whom more can be added when necessary. The permanent staff of a well-run opera house is necessarily large. If the theatre functions full-time throughout the season, it will also need administrative staff, musical staff including conductors, coaches, rehearsal pianists, a music librarian and other skilled workers such as carpenters to make the sets, people to

**the economics
of opera** make and maintain the costumes, electricians and, of course, the front of house staff which any theatre requires.

All this costs a large amount of money. If the expense had to be recovered totally from box office takings, we would have to pay two or three times as much for our seats at the opera as we pay at present.

Fortunately, in most countries the state subsidises the leading opera companies. In Germany and Austria, the leading theatres, such as the Deutsche Oper in Berlin, and the Vienna State Opera, are generously supported by the state. In Great Britain, we have fewer opera companies, and they are inadequately subsidised in comparison with the theatres of most other European countries. In the United States, subsidy comes mostly from private and business sources.

In Great Britain, though rarely elsewhere in the world, non-opera-going tax-payers are sometimes heard to complain about the large subsidies which are paid to opera companies, because in their view, opera is an élitist and expensive art form enjoyed only by the aristocracy and well-heeled snobs. This is demonstrably untrue, and in any case these same tax-payers do not think to complain about the cost of art galleries, museums, public libraries and many other amenities used only by a minority of the population. It is very important for opera, as a major art form, that there should be at least one national company in each country which is able to maintain the highest possible standards. The big companies must plan their productions several years in advance so that they can secure the services of star singers and conductors. And it is equally important that opera companies, like drama companies, should flourish at regional and local levels as well.

It is not easy to give even an approximate idea of the cost of a new production of an opera at, for instance, the Royal Opera House in London, for costs vary so much and for so many reasons. Clearly, some operas are more expensive to stage than others. Verdi's *Don Carlos* or Strauss's *Die Frau ohne Schatten* have larger casts and require bigger orchestral resources than Mozart's *Così fan tutte.* But you should bear in mind that, quite apart from such overhead costs as the cleaning and heating of the theatre, front-of-house and backstage staffs, several elements have to be paid for every time an opera is staged. A conductor and international soloists can cost thousands of pounds per performance. Add to that the fees for supporting singers, chorus and orchestra, and the cost of the evening could be about £40,000. A theatre seating 2000 people will need to sell all of its seats at an average price of £20 to come anywhere near breaking even. It would, in fact, sell its best seats at nearly double that price, and make some cheaper seats available. Subsidy, whether from the state or from private enterprise, will help to keep the costs and therefore the seat prices down. Do not forget that to the cost of each performance should be added some portion of the actual costs of the original production. The producer and the designer of sets and costumes will have been paid a fee, and the sets and costumes will have cost money to originate. These production costs can easily total £200,000 or more – though an opera can be put on for as little as £10,000.

**the economics
of opera**

3

WHERE TO FIND OPERA

opera in Britain

Operas today do not have to take place in lavishly equipped nineteenth-century opera houses, nor do they have to be performed in unfamiliar languages. Opera is much more accessible. You can find it in local theatres and in concert halls. You can find it sung in the original language or in English translation. You can watch it on television with sub-titles, and even in the cinema. You can listen to it as often as you like on long-playing records and cassettes.

The leading opera company in Great Britain is the Royal Opera, which performs at the Royal Opera House, Covent Garden, London, for nine or ten months of the year. The Royal Opera is generally reckoned to be one of the leading four or five opera companies of international standard in the world today. The others include the Metropolitan Opera in New York, the Vienna State Opera, La Scala, Milan, and, arguably, the Paris Opera and the Bolshoi in Moscow. The Royal Opera shares its theatre with the Royal Ballet, but during the season from September to July there are at least three performances of opera each week. Throughout a season, approximately twenty operas will be performed, and there may be five or six performances of each opera. The repertory is usually well-balanced, including works by the five most popular composers (Mozart, Verdi, Wagner, Puccini and Strauss) as well as one or two novelties.

England's second full-time opera company is the English National Opera (ENO), housed at the London Coliseum. Whereas the Royal Opera usually performs works in their original languages, mainly because it uses a number of guest artists from abroad who can be expected to know their roles only in the languages in which they were written, the policy of the English National Opera is to perform operas in English translation, and to employ, for the most part, British and Commonwealth singers. The managements of these two major companies attempt to avoid duplication of repertoire, though there are some extremely popular works which it is useful to have available both in the original language and in the vernacular.

An offshoot of English National Opera is ENO North, based at the Grand Theatre, Leeds, which plays for a few weeks of the year in its home town and tours to other centres in the north of England.

Both Scotland and Wales maintain opera companies: Scottish Opera based in Glasgow and Welsh National Opera based in Cardiff. Both these companies tour for part of the year, not only in their own countries but also in England. Another useful touring company is Kent Opera, whose resources are more modest than those of its rivals but whose standards are high. Tours are also undertaken by Opera 80, which was set up by the Arts Council to bring opera to towns lacking theatres large enough to attract the major touring companies.

A special case is Glyndebourne Festival Opera. This company plays in the summer months in a specially-built theatre in the house of the Christie family at Glyndebourne, near Lewes, Sussex. Begun in 1934 by John Christie, Glyndebourne Opera is now run by his son, George Christie, with subsidy from private and business sources. Four or five operas are produced each summer, and the standards of production

opera in Britain

and musical preparation are high. A subsidiary is Glyndebourne Touring Opera which tours the operas after they have first been seen at the Glyndebourne theatre. The touring operation is helped financially through being engaged by the Arts Council to supplement the tours of the subsidised companies.

Opera also plays an important role in some of the music festivals which take place throughout the year, most notably at the internationally renowned Edinburgh Festival where companies from abroad are often to be heard. The Aldeburgh Festival specialises in the operas of Benjamin Britten, and the re-opening of the Buxton Opera House in Derbyshire has led to the appearance of a new Buxton Opera festival which may, in time, come to rival Glyndebourne. In Ireland, the enterprising festival at Wexford every autumn stages three operas, of which at least two are usually rarities, revivals of operas not seen for some years and thus due for re-appraisal.

You can obtain information about performances in your area by writing to your Regional Arts Association. Often, group visits are organised with reductions on the price of tickets and travel.

If there is an opera company in your vicinity, it probably has a supporters' club, with lectures and various activities designed to spread information about opera. There are also, of course, a number of amateur opera clubs and societies which welcome not only singers and musicians but also interested and enthusiastic people willing to help backstage or front-of-house, or in some other capacity.

There is a very good monthly magazine called *Opera,* which is not only full of interesting articles about operas and singers, but also contains up-to-date news and advance information about opera performances in most parts of the world, as well as reviews of performances in Great Britain, Europe, America and elsewhere. (I ought to declare an interest: I am a member of the Editorial Board of *Opera.* However, the Board is not paid a salary; we give our time out of our interest in and love of the art of opera.) The excellent American magazine, *Opera News,* published by the Metropolitan Opera Guild, can be obtained on subscription.

opera abroad

opera
abroad

In Germany and Austria, most towns have their own civic opera companies, performing opera and operetta throughout the year, with the exception of two months in high summer. However, it is possible to encounter summer performances of opera and operetta in a number of holiday resorts.

If one wishes to base a holiday on going to the opera abroad, some information about the major international companies may be useful. For instance, it is no use going to Milan in the summer and expecting to find La Scala Opera House open and functioning. The opera season in Milan is confined to the winter months, as it is throughout Italy. La Scala traditionally opens on 7 December every year, and offers one or two performances each week until March. What Italy provides in the summer is outdoor opera. This can be found at the magnificent Arena in Verona, the Caracalla Baths in Rome and in Puccini's village of Torre del Lago. The standard in Verona is consistently high, but in Rome and Torre del Lago it varies.

The opera-goer is on safer ground in Vienna where two opera houses, the State Opera and the Volksoper (roughly equivalent to London's Royal Opera and English National Opera), function seven nights a week for ten months of the year, closing only in July and August when many of the singers and conductors will be found performing at the prestigious and highly expensive Salzburg Festival. In May and June, during the Vienna Festival, there are often visits from foreign opera companies in addition to the usual fare.

In Germany, the opera season in Munich is a lengthy one, and the summer festival there concentrates on operas by Strauss, Wagner and Mozart.

In America, the Metropolitan Opera and the New York City Opera are usually to be found operating in New York during the autumn and winter months. In spring, the Metropolitan (or Met) goes on tour. The United States has a number of first-class opera companies, among them the Lyric Opera of Chicago and the San Francisco Opera. There is an opera festival in the summer months in Santa Fé, New Mexico, and in California the San Diego Opera also mounts a summer festival, devoted to the operas of Verdi.

radio, television and video

In addition to the hundreds of complete recordings of operas which are now available (see pages 83 to 141) and the many radio broadcasts, a welcome development in recent years has been the transmission of opera performances on television. Some of these programmes are produced in television studios, but most of them are relayed directly from the opera houses. In Britain it is now possible to see on television performances from New York and Vienna as well as from the Royal Opera House or from Glyndebourne. Television screenings, and the growing number of video cassettes of opera now available, are expecially useful when operas sung in the original languages are accompanied by sub-titles flashed on to the screen. This is an ideal way to become acquainted with an unfamiliar opera in an unfamiliar language. A major event in televised opera in Great Britain was the screening of Wagner's complete *Ring* in 1982.

4

THE LANGUAGE OF OPERA

The question of language is one which seems to divide opinion, and sometimes quite fiercely. Those who prefer their opera in the original language occasionally vent their scorn, in the correspondence columns of the musical magazines, on English-language performances of foreign operas, while the supporters of opera in English denounce their opponents as snobs. I am not averse to an argument, when the cause is right, but I have never thought it necessary to take sides on this particular issue. Ideally, of course, an opera should be heard in the language in which the composer set the words. The sound as well as the sense of the words has caused him to write those particular notes. If the composer knows his business, he will avoid asking singers to sing very high or very low notes on vowel sounds which can cause difficulty. Dame Joan Sutherland projects a stunning high E flat, but I doubt if she could do so while singing an 'oo' sound in any language ('moon', 'luna', 'lumière' or 'Bruder').

However, no one understands every language under the sun. Among the hundreds of languages I do not understand is Czechoslovakian. Am I to deny myself the pleasure of hearing and understanding Smetana's delightful opera, *The Bartered Bride*? For that matter, my knowledge of Russian is virtually non-existent. Must I stay away from *Boris Godunov* by Mussorgsky? I do not stay away from Dostoevsky: I read *Crime and Punishment* and *The Brothers Karamazov* in English, also the poems of Pushkin. Something may be lost in the translation, but what I get is considerably better than nothing. Having heard several performances of *Boris Godunov* or Tchaikovsky's *Eugene Onegin* in English, I now know these operas sufficiently well to listen to them in Russian. An alternative approach is to listen to an original-language recording and follow it with a score which contains an English translation for singing. Most record companies include, with the discs, a libretto in the original language and in English.

When it comes to operas sung in languages I can understand (English, French, German, Italian), I do prefer to hear them well sung in the original language; but I can derive almost as much enjoyment from a first-class performance in English, if the translation is good. Some operas translate better than others; some languages translate better into English than others. And singers, however cosmopolitan they may be, are usually more confident in their own language: Rita Hunter in English and in German might almost be two different singers, and the same could be said of Kiri Te Kanawa. Gwyneth Jones, however, sounds as much at ease in German as in English, and Geraint Evans's Italian rolls naturally off his tongue in the Mozart comedies.

So, listen to opera in any language you like. If the only language you like is English, do not be bullied by the 'original language at all costs' brigade. But, if you prefer your opera in its own tongue, don't be afraid of being thought snobbish. You *are* snobbish only if you persist in sitting through operas in languages you do not understand; in which case you are not only snobbish but foolish because you are cutting yourself off from a much greater enjoyment of the opera.

However well you know the music and *think* you know the plot, in synopsis form, of a popular opera which you may have seen several times, you will not derive anywhere near total enjoyment of all that it has to offer until you understand, line by line, what the characters are saying or singing to

Elizabeth Pruett as Donna Elvira and Richard van Allan as
Leporello in a scene from Peter Hall's production of Mozart's
Don Giovanni at Glyndebourne Festival Opera.

A scene from the English National Opera production
of Puccini's *La Bohème*.

one another. Let me illustrate this point, using the most familiar opera I can think of, *La Bohème.* Of course you know the story. Who doesn't? In Act I, the Bohemians mess around with a great deal of horseplay, then Rodolfo meets the consumptive Mimi. In Act II, Rodolfo introduces Mimi to his friends at the Café Momus, and one of his friends, Marcello, meets up again with a somewhat flashy lady from his past, Musetta. In Act III, Mimi and Rodolfo have decided to part, and they do so regretfully. In Act IV, the Bohemian artists are larking about in their studio when Musetta rushes in to say that Mimi is ill and dying. Mimi is brought in, attempts are made to procure medicine for her, but she dies. End of opera.

You may think that with no more knowledge than this of what is happening on the stage, and Puccini's luscious melodies sweeping over you, you are getting as much as you can out of *La Bohème.* But if that is what you think, you are mistaken. Even the clowning of the Bohemians in Acts I and IV is more interesting if you know what they are saying to one another. This is so obviously true that it is in danger of being overlooked: you are not properly experiencing an opera, a play with music, unless you listen to the words as well as the music, or to be more accurate the words which are carried by the music. Let us look at the first scene of *La Bohème* up to the entrance of Benoit, the landlord. In my synopsis above, it is included in the phrase 'The Bohemians mess around with a great deal of horseplay'. But, below, I have roughly translated the actual dialogue.

(The scene is an attic in Montparnasse in Paris, somewhere around 1830. It is winter. Two friends are at work, Marcello who is a painter, and Rodolfo a poet and playwright.)

Marcello: This 'Red Sea' painting of mine makes me feel as cold as though I were immersed in the sea itself. I'll take my revenge by drowning a Pharaoh. (*To Rodolfo, who is looking out of a window*) What are you doing?

Rodolfo: I'm looking at the Paris sky, grimy with the smoke of a thousand chimneys, and I'm thinking about this wretched old stove of ours which is as idle as a man of leisure.

Marcello:	Ah well, it's a long time since we fed him properly.
Rodolfo:	Why are all those stupid forests covered with snow?
Marcello:	Rodolfo, I'm going to tell you one of my very profound thoughts. I'm absolutely freezing.
Rodolfo:	And I shan't keep any secrets from you, Marcello: I don't believe I'm actually sweating.
Marcello:	My fingers are as frozen as if I had plunged them into that great frozen space, the heart of Musetta. (*He sighs and leaves off painting*)
Rodolfo:	Love is a stove that burns too much . . .
Marcello:	And too fast!
Rodolfo:	Where man is the fuel . . .
Marcello:	And woman the spark.
Rodolfo:	The one burns in an instant . . .
Marcello:	And the other stands, watching.
Rodolfo:	But in the meantime we're freezing here . . .
Marcello:	And dying of hunger.
Rodolfo:	We must have a fire.
Marcello:	(*seizing a chair*) Hold on, we'll sacrifice the chair!
Rodolfo:	(*stops him, then shouts for joy*) Eureka!
Marcello:	You've thought of something?
Rodolfo:	Yes. Sharpen your wits, and let your thoughts burst into flame.
Marcello:	(*pointing to his painting*) Shall we burn the Red Sea?
Rodolfo:	No. Painted canvas would smell too much. What about my play? The fierce intensity of my drama will warm us.
Marcello:	You're going to read it aloud? I'll freeze!
Rodolfo:	No. The paper will turn to ashes, and my genius will float back to heaven whence it came. This will be a great loss to the century, but when Rome is in danger . . .
Marcello:	Oh, generous-hearted one!
Rodolfo:	You take Act One. (*Handing it to him*)
Marcello:	Right.

Rodolfo: Tear it up.

Marcello: Set it alight. (*Rodolfo puts part of the manuscript in the stove, and lights it. Then the two friends take chairs, and sit close to the stove, basking in the warmth*)

Both: What blissful heat. (*The door opens noisily, and Colline enters, stamping his feet with cold. He throws a bundle of books on to the table*)

Colline: Already there are portents of the Apocalypse. The pawnshops don't function on Christmas Eve. (*Surprised*) A fire!

Rodolfo: Quiet! My play is being given . . .

Marcello: . . . to the flames.

Colline: I find it scintillating.

Rodolfo: Lively.

Marcello: But not very long.

Rodolfo: There's great merit in brevity.

Colline: Author, may I have the chair?

Marcello: One can die of boredom in these intervals. Hurry up!

Rodolfo: Act Two.

Marcello: No whispering.

Colline: What profundity of thought.

Marcello: And so colourful.

Rodolfo: There's an ardent love scene dying in that bright blue flame.

Colline: How that page crackles.

Marcello: Those were the kisses.

Rodolfo: I'd like to hear the remaining three acts together. (*Throws the rest of the manuscript on the flames*)

Colline: Such unity of concept is quite audacious.

All: What a beautiful death scene in that joyous flame. (*They applaud. Then the flame dies down*)

Marcello: My God, the flame is dying!

Colline: What a useless drama, so fragile.

Marcello: Already curling up to die.

Colline and Marcello:	Down with the author!
	(*Two boys enter, one carrying food, bottles of wine, and cigars, and the other a bundle of wood. Hearing them come in, the three men turn around from the stove and fall upon the provisions with shouts of amazement*)
Rodolfo:	Wood!
Marcello:	Cigars!
Colline:	Claret!
Rodolfo:	Wood!
Marcello:	Claret!
All:	Destiny provides us with a great feast. (*The boys leave, and Schaunard enters with an air of triumph, scattering coins on the floor*)
Schaunard:	The Bank of France opens its coffers to you.
Colline:	(*as he and the others pick up the coins*) Pick them up, pick them up!
Marcello:	They're pieces of tin.
Schaunard:	Are you deaf? Are you bleary-eyed? (*Shows Marcello a coin*) Who is this man?
Rodolfo:	(*looking at it*) Louis Philippe! I bow to my King!
All:	Louis Philippe is at our feet!
Schaunard:	Now I'll tell you. This gold, or rather this silver, has quite a story attached to it.
Rodolfo:	Let's heat the stove.
Colline:	I've suffered so much from the cold.
Schaunard:	An Englishman – a gentleman – a Lord, or whatever – was seeking a musician –
Marcello:	Come on, let's set the table!
Schaunard:	And I? I flew to him!
Rodolfo:	Where's the food?
Colline:	Here.
Marcello:	Take it.

Schaunard:	I present myself to him. He accepts me, and I ask him:
Colline:	Cold roast beef!
Marcello:	Pastries!
Schaunard:	'When shall we begin the lessons?' He replies 'Let's start now'. (*Schaunard imitates an upper-class English accent*) 'Look!' And he points out to me a parrot on the ground floor, then adds 'You must keep on playing until that bird dies!'
Rodolfo:	Our dining-room looks brilliant.
Schaunard:	And that's how it was. I played for three long days –
Marcello:	Now the candles.
Colline:	Those pastries!
Schaunard:	Then I employed the charm of my handsome figure, and fascinated the serving-maid –
Marcello:	Must we eat without a table-cloth?
Rodolfo:	No, I've got an idea. (*Takes a newspaper from his pocket*)
Marcello and Colline:	The *Constitutional!*
Rodolfo:	An excellent paper. One can devour both food and news.
Schaunard	We poisoned a little parsley, Lorito spread his wings, opened his beak, just a little sprig of parsley and he died like Socrates!
Colline:	Who?
Schaunard:	Go to the devil, all of you. Now what are you up to? (*as he sees them about to eat*) No! These delicacies are our insurance against gloomy and obscure days in the future. What, dine at home on Christmas Eve, when the Latin Quarter has decked its streets with sausages and other eatables? When the fragrance of fritters perfumes the air of the ancient streets? There, where the young girls sing happily . . .
All:	It's Christmas Eve!
Schaunard:	And the song of each girl is echoed by her student boyfriend? We shall drink at home, but we shall dine out.
	(*They are pouring the wine, when there is a knock at the door*)

All of that dialogue takes place in the first few minutes of *La Bohème*. It is quite clear that, with even so popular and well-known an opera, one's enjoyment of a performance in a foreign language is greatly enhanced if one takes the trouble to read a translation first. It need not take long. One can easily read through *La Bohème* in twenty minutes. Reading up on the original work from which the opera is derived is the logical extension of this. Henri Murger's novel, *The Bohemians*, exists in English translation and is a delightful book, rather like a French *Pickwick Papers.*

In the case of operas involving real historical characters, a knowledge of the historical background will also add to one's appreciation of the opera. For instance, to someone about to attend a performance of Verdi's *Don Carlos* for the first time, I would say (a) read the libretto; (b) read Schiller's play, *Don Carlos,* on which the opera is based – there are English translations of it; (c) read a popular work on Philip II of Spain and the Spanish Inquisition. At the very least, read something about the opera and the circumstances of its composition. See 'Suggestions for Further Reading' on page 156.

5

EARLY
OPERAS

We do not know very much about the drama of ancient Greece, although some of its plays have survived. However, we do know that music played a considerable part in it – in the chanting of the choruses and in the interpolation of songs into the action. The old Greek dramas were, in a sense, the earliest operas. With the decline of the Greek civilisation music disappeared from the theatre for several centuries. When it came back, it did so via the church.

In mediaeval times, a kind of play or dramatic dialogue began to appear in the churches. These Easter Sepulchre Plays, dramatising the Passion and resurrection of Christ, were performed with music, and from them other sacred plays with music developed – Christmas dramas, episodes from the gospel accounts of the life of Christ and Old Testament stories. One Old Testament play, *The Play of Daniel*, has come down to us. Written and composed in the twelfth century, it is the earliest surviving forerunner of what we know today as opera.

Gradually during the Middle Ages, the plays with music began to emerge from the church and to be performed in secular surroundings. Freed from the restrictions of church performance, the writers were able to extend their range of subjects and the language in which those subjects were treated. Over the years, the musical element in the plays began to diminish, and the spoken dialogue took on a greater complexity. From this background, the spoken theatre developed. Music developed separately, both instrumentally and vocally.

the Camerata

It was not until the very end of the sixteenth century, in Florence, that music and spoken drama were brought together again. This was achieved by the Camerata, a group of Florentine scholars, poets and musicians who, for some years, met at the houses of Giovanni Bardi and Count Vernio, and later at that of Jacopo Corsi. The group did not set out to invent 'opera'. What happened was that, out of their discussions of the problems relating to the arts in their time, there grew a desire to revive the tragic drama of classical Greek and Roman antiquity. They wanted to restore music to the role they conceived it to have held at that time, and to this end they began to experiment in the setting of words to music for dramatic purposes. In fact, the Camerata was by no means exclusively or even predominantly musical, but its members included musicians, such as the composers Jacopo Peri and Giulio Caccini, and the poet Ottavio Rinuccini who wrote some of the first texts for the new dramas with music. Another member of the circle was Vincenzo Galilei, father of the great astronomer.

The first full-scale opera did not emerge immediately from the Camerata's discussions and experiments. Short cantatas, compositions for solo voice accompanied either by one instrument or by a small group of instruments, were the first works to appear. One such work was Caccini's *Le Nuove musiche,* a collection of simple melodies, whose title – New Music – was soon used to describe the movement represented by the Camerata. It was a musical style in which the word was all-important, or conversely it was a method of setting speech so as to give the speech rhythm and variations of pitch for emphasis.

The first recognisable opera was *Dafne,* with music by Peri and text by Rinuccini. Its subject was taken, as was the case with most of the early operas, from classical mythology. Daphne, the daughter of the river-god Peneus, loved by Apollo, is metamorphosed into a laurel tree. The music of Peri's *Dafne,* which was first performed in Jacopo Corsi's house in Florence in 1597, has been lost, but the success of the experiment was such that, in 1600, Peri was given the opportunity to produce a similar work for the festivities which followed the marriage of Henri IV of France with Maria de' Medici. For this occasion, he composed a work for the stage, *Euridice,* which is the acknowledged prototype of the modern opera.

Euridice, with music by Peri and text again by Rinuccini, is the earliest opera of which the music is extant. (It was revived for the first time in the twentieth century at Saratoga Springs, New York, in 1941. More recently, it has been recorded.) We know something of the conditions of its first performance, at the Pitti Palace in Florence, in which several members of the nobility took part; Jacopo Corsi presided at the harpsichord, three friends played string instruments, and at one point in the score three flutes appear to have joined in. The orchestra, therefore, was small and the interest was centred upon the human voices and upon the characters of the drama.

It is not easy to understand the excitement which was engendered by this new art form, for *Euridice* today sounds rather dull to those of us who are not specialists in the period. This is because the music is mostly in what was called recitative style, recitative being what one might call musical prose as opposed to musical poetry. When the characters declaim speeches or dialogue in a kind of heightened speech or chant which has no melodic interest, that is recitative. Its rhythms follow those of natural speech, and so, to a certain extent, do the rise and fall of its notes. The words dictate the notes, whereas in melody the notes often bend the words to their own rhythm and pitch.

Monteverdi

Monteverdi

After the Florentine Camerata had shown the way ahead, composers in other parts of Italy began to experiment with opera. In Rome, Emilio de' Cavalieri produced his opera, *La Rappresentazione di anima e di corpo*, in 1600, the same year as *Euridice*, and he was soon followed by a number of other Roman composers. The Roman school reached the peak of its achievement in 1634 with *Il Sant' Alessio* by Stefano Landi. But it was in Mantua, in 1607, that the first great genius of Italian opera emerged, when Claudio Monteverdi, music master to the court of Vincenzo Gonzaga, Duke of Mantua, composed his *Arianna*.

The story of *Arianna* is based on the legend of Ariadne, who saved Theseus from the Minotaur's labyrinth but was later abandoned by him on the island of Naxos. (The most famous operatic treatment of the myth is a twentieth-century opera, Richard Strauss's *Ariadne auf Naxos*.) The scene in which Ariadne bewails the departure of her faithless lover produced an extraordinary effect upon the audience. The expressive power of Monteverdi's music can still be experienced, for Ariadne's lament 'Lasciatemi morire' (Leave me to die) is one of the few portions of the opera to have been preserved.

Monteverdi's *Arianna* was so successful that the composer was immediately invited to compose another opera. This time, he chose the story of Orpheus and Euridice, as Peri had done seven years earlier in Florence. Monteverdi's *La Favola d'Orfeo* uses a much larger orchestra than Peri's *Euridice*, and its recitative is dramatically expressive. With this opera, Monteverdi's vocal style begins to move towards greater melodic interest. The voices not only carry the dramatic action forward through recitative but also reflect on events and express their feelings in music of a type which is half-way between the prose of recitative and the poetry of the tuneful aria. This is called *arioso* style.

Opposite: Anne Howells as the goddess Minerva in the Glyndebourne Festival Opera production of *Il Ritorno d'Ulisse in patria* (The Return of Ulysses to his country) by Monteverdi.

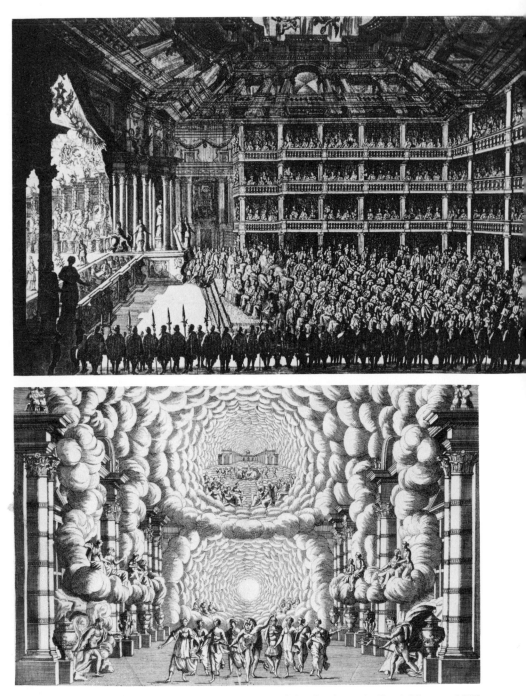

Top: A performance of *Il Pomo d'Oro* by Antonio Cesti, Vienna, 1667.
Below: *Le Nozze di Peleó e di Teti* by Carlo Coproli, designed by
Jiaicomo Torelli da Fano and performed at the Opéra, Paris, in 1654.

seventeenth-century audiences

seventeenth-
century
audiences

In its early days, opera was an especially lavish and expensive entertainment, usually staged only in connection with some festivity or other, its costs underwritten by a prince or potentate. Performances took place in private theatres, many of them erected for the occasion.

Towards the middle of the seventeenth century, opera began to be accessible to the public at large. The first public opera house was opened in Venice with an opera by the Venetian composer Cavalli, and by the end of the century there were at least half a dozen opera houses in that city, where most of Cavalli's forty-two operas were performed. With the widening of the opera public came also greater diversity in the plots of operas. The Venetian audiences, for instance, were less interested in classical legends than in operas about real human beings. As a result, the love interest in the operas became less stylised, and a comic element began to achieve greater prominence. From what we read of the period, most important of all were the fantastic scenic effects engineered by the architects and designers of the baroque age.

the spread of opera

This new Italian entertainment did not take long to spread beyond the borders of Italy. The Imperial court at Vienna, in those days the most resplendent in Europe, staged Italian operas on the most lavish scale imaginable, and smaller courts throughout the German-speaking countries followed the Viennese example. In Paris, the opera took longer to establish itself, not only because French composers were bitterly jealous of the Italians but also because of the long-established tradition in France of the court masque, with its emphasis on the dance. When French composers such as Lully (who was, in fact, Italian-born) turned to the art form, it was to produce a hybrid opera-ballet from which the great period of French *grand opéra,* with its strong element of ballet, would eventually flower.

If opera did not establish itself as quickly in England as on the Continent, this was largely due to the Civil War and the years of Puritan rule. After the Restoration, plays with incidental music and songs began to appear on the stages of the re-opened playhouses, as well as adaptations of the plays of Shakespeare with elements of the masque and of dancing introduced. *The Tempest* was the most successful of these. Purcell's *King Arthur,* staged in 1691 with text by Dryden, was thought of as an opera, though most of its principal characters do not sing and its musical and dramatic aspects are kept fairly separate. The first real English opera, and Purcell's only true opera, was *Dido and Aeneas,* produced in 1689, not in a professional theatre but in a school for young ladies in Chelsea. Though its setting of the English language was masterly, and Purcell's music really interpreted the drama in a way in which earlier incidental music in the English theatre had barely attempted, *Dido and Aeneas* was not immediately followed by other English operas. In fact, the English musical stage had to wait two hundred years for any comparable works of genius.

It was Italian opera, opera sung in Italian, which established itself as a fashionable entertainment in London in the eighteenth century, and which was to be heard in most other European countries as well.

In some German towns, however, a native-language opera also began to emerge. The first permanent opera company in the German-speaking states was opened in Hamburg as early as 1678, and it was there that German-language opera began to establish itself. Reinhard Keiser was the earliest Hamburg opera composer of any note, and he exercised a strong influence upon the eighteen-year-old Handel who arrived in Hamburg from his native Halle in 1703.

What had happened throughout the seventeenth century, then, was that opera was born in Italy, and established itself in Italian. Despite the fact that during the century operas were written in other languages, among them French, German and English, to most people opera meant Italian opera. Begun by a small group of aristocratic intellectuals in Florence, many of whom were amateurs, opera was taken over by the professional musicians and poets, and gradually became

popular with a middle-class public as well as with the wealthy
classes who had initially supported it. The tendency, from the
very beginning, was for opera to deal with subjects remote
from daily life. Even when it began to take subjects from
sources other than the myths of classical Greece and Rome,
opera did not attempt realistic subjects of its own day, nor did
it take too easily to low comedy or farce. Opera in the seventeenth century dealt with life's poetry, not with its prose.

**the spread
of opera**

With the arguable exception of Purcell's *Dido and
Aeneas*, which is still, and understandably, of interest to
English audiences, the operas of the seventeenth century are
not likely to attract the average opera-goer, despite the occasional resplendent revival under festival conditions at Glyndebourne and elsewhere, for they are melodically weak.

6

OPERA
IN THE
EIGHTEENTH
CENTURY

By the beginning of the eighteenth century most great European cities supported opera houses; but, except in Paris, all the operas produced were in Italian, whether or not they were composed by Italians. Italian had become the language of music, not only because opera had begun in Italy, but because Italian musicians had infiltrated into the musical life of Europe generally. In Italy the leading composer at the beginning of the century was Alessandro Scarlatti, and it is with him that modern opera could be said properly to have begun.

By the time of Scarlatti, opera had developed sufficiently for the composer to be able to reject the monotony of the old recitative and strike out on a new path, using recitative much more sparsely and making the aria the most important element in the complete work.

Scarlatti's ground-plan called for ordinary recitative, accompanied only by harpsichord (*recitativo secco*, literally 'dry recitative'), to be used for ordinary dialogue; orchestrally accompanied recitative (*recitativo stromentato*) for the expression of violent emotion; and the aria for soliloquy or reflection. Scarlatti also stereotyped the aria by giving it what

has come to be known as a-b-a form, 'b' consisting of a con-
trasted middle section which is followed by a return of the
opening section 'a'. This eventually led to a deadening formality, but for a great part of the eighteenth century composers were able to breathe exciting dramatic life into this
form. The arias eventually became too elaborate and too much
the vehicle for display on the part of the singer. Reform of
some kind thus became a necessity.

Handel, who had begun his operatic career in Hamburg with German opera, went to Italy in 1706 at the age of
twenty-one and began to write Italian operas with great facility. His first Italian opera, *Rodrigo,* produced in Florence in
1707, was followed by *Agrippina,* staged in Venice in 1709. A
year or two later, Handel moved to London where he was to
spend the greater part of his creative life, and where, for many
years, he continued to compose operas in Italian, among them
Padamisto (1720), *Giulio Cesare* (1724) and *Alcina* (1735). By
1741, he had produced about forty operas for London theatres,
in almost all of which he made use of the conventions of
Italian opera as performed in Italy. One of the most remarkable of these was the convention of the male soprano. It had
been the custom of the church in Italy (a custom which
remained alive until the end of the nineteenth century) to pre-
serve the male soprano voice beyond puberty, through castra-
tion. Adult *castrati* began to sing the leading male roles in
opera. Dramatic verisimilitude suffered, but the *castrati* were
renowned for their virtuosity. Composers shaped arias to suit
their individual talents, and audiences flocked to hear them.

The title-role of Julius Caesar in Handel's *Giulio
Cesare* was written for a castrato. When this opera is staged
today, there being no male adult sopranos on offer, the man-
agement can cast either a male (usually a baritone) or a
soprano (invariably a female) or a male counter-tenor (i.e. a
normal adult male singing falsetto). Even after *castrati* ceased
to appear in opera, composers occasionally wrote male roles
(usually pubescent or adolescent males) to be sung by
(female) sopranos: Siebel in Gounod's *Faust* (1859) is one such
role, and another is Octavian in Richard Strauss's *Der Rosenkavalier* (1911).

In France, Italian customs did not take hold. Lully and

his followers Campra and Destouches created a distinctly French opera which was to influence Rameau, who became the most admired composer of opera in France. His subjects were chiefly classical, as were those of Italian opera, but the chorus played a more important part than the solo aria, and ballet played a still larger role. Throughout the eighteenth century opera in France continued to go its own way.

comic opera

Of the operas we have so far considered, the earliest were composed for court theatres, and all were conceived with highly educated audiences in mind. The low farce of the popular spoken theatre had no place in opera, nor to any appreciable extent did comedy of any kind, elevated or low. But during the eighteenth century a genre of comic opera became popular. It began quite modestly in Naples with operas in local dialect which dealt with everyday themes and characters, some of them full-length operas and others no more than interludes to be performed between the acts of more serious operas.

One of these shorter pieces which has survived and is still performed today is Pergolesi's *La Serva padrona* (The Maid as Mistress), first staged in 1733. *La Serva padrona* was brought to London by a comic opera troupe from Naples in 1740 where it was enthusiastically received, but it was only when Paris heard it in 1752 that Pergolesi's agreeable comedy really made its effect. French audiences found it a delightful and much needed change from the stately grandeur of Rameau, and Pergolesi soon had his disciples and imitators in France. Other comic operas from Naples and Venice began to be staged in Paris. For some time in France comic opera both in French and in Italian proved extremely popular, the French composers tending to separate the musical numbers by spoken dialogue while the Italians continued to use sung recitative.

Comic opera had been seen in England even before Pergolesi showed how it was done in Italy. *The Beggar's Opera*, a satire on Italian opera, had been staged in London in

1728. This was really a play with songs and occasional choruses, rather than an opera, but it was quite close in style to the
developing French *opéra comique*. Its dialogue was by John
Gay, and its music was arranged by John Pepusch, a German
musician who worked in London theatres. Pepusch took his
tunes from the popular songs of the day, as well as from Purcell and Handel. He also made use of folk tunes from France
and Germany, but he orchestrated them in such a way that
they took on a new and original character. The success of *The
Beggar's Opera* led to an enormous number of other 'ballad
operas', as they came to be called in England, and these in
turn made their way to Germany where they strongly
influenced the emerging German comic opera movement.

comic opera

Gluck and opera reform

The serious opera, in the form in which Alessandro Scarlatti
had left it, had become the prisoner of its own conventions.
Unless the art form was to become moribund, there was a
need for reform, and this reform would perhaps have been
undertaken earlier in the eighteenth century had not the crisis
affecting opera been obscured by the genius of Handel, who
kept the old-style opera alive in its last years. The reformer,
when he finally arrived in the second half of the century, was
not an Italian composer, but a German of Bohemian stock,
Christoph Willibald von Gluck. Gluck, generally regarded as
opera's second founder, began his career as a composer of
conventional eighteenth-century opera but eventually
became dissatisfied with a situation whereby the composer
appeared to be the servant of the leading singers.

With *Orfeo ed Euridice* (Orpheus and Eurydice), produced in Vienna in 1762, Gluck and his librettist Calzabigi
brought a new kind of opera into being, an opera in which the
music followed not the whims of the singers but the dictates of
the drama, and in which arias and choruses were given a new
freedom of form and a consequent intensification of expression. *Orfeo ed Euridice* is the oldest opera which survives in the
international operatic repertoire of today, not as a rarity to be

Gluck and opera reform

occasionally exhumed and examined, but as a popular and living work.

Gluck went on to write a number of other Italian operas, among them *Alceste* (1767) and *Paride ed Elena* (Paris and Helen: 1770) before turning his attention to French opera. For Paris he composed *Iphigénie en Aulide* (Iphigenia in Aulis: 1774) and *Armide* (1777) among others, as well as arranging *Orfeo ed Euridice* and adapting it to a French text as *Orphée et Eurydice*, with the role of Orpheus, originally written for male contralto, now assigned to a high tenor.

The production of Gluck's operas in Paris touched off an artistic rivalry with Piccinni, an Italian composer who was popular in Paris. But, popular though he was, Piccinni proved no match for Gluck, though the feud between their respective supporters continued long after Gluck had retired to Vienna.

Mozart

Vienna, in the second half of the eighteenth century, had already become the musical capital of Europe, with a lively and varied musical life and a flourishing opera company. When the young Salzburg composer, Wolfgang Amadeus Mozart, took up residence in Vienna in 1781, he had already composed more than a dozen operas, though his greatest works in opera were to be composed during the ten years of life remaining to him.

Mozart composed his first operas while he was still a child, among them the comic opera *La Finta semplice* (The Feigned Idiot-Girl) which he wrote when he was twelve, and *Mitridate, Re di Ponto* (Mithridates, King of Pontus), composed for Milan when he was fourteen. *La Finta giardiniera* (The Feigned Garden-Maid) was composed for Munich when he was only nineteen. Mozart's greatest achievement in opera before he came to Vienna, *Idomeneo*, was also composed for Munich, in his twenty-fifth year.

With *Idomeneo*, Mozart brought a new and greater humanity to the classical world of *opera seria*, serious opera. With the operas that were to follow, he raised the entire art form to a higher level, by the genius of his musicianship and

his extraordinary skill in musical characterisation. After put-
ting German-language opera on its feet with *Die Entführung
aus dem Serail* (The Abduction from the Harem) in 1782,
Mozart then proceeded to produce, with the Italian poet
Lorenzo da Ponte as his librettist, three great masterpieces of
Italian opera: *Le Nozze di Figaro* (The Marriage of Figaro),
Don Giovanni and *Così fan tutte* (All women are like that).
The old recitatives and arias were transformed, and the writ-
ing for ensembles had a complexity which was at the same
time natural and spontaneous.

Mozart is the first great modern musical dramatist. In
the operas of his adolescence, he merely wrote strings of
beautiful arias, but by the time he embarked upon *Le Nozze
di Figaro* (1786) he had learned how to use his music to
express character and to adapt to a given dramatic situation.
Figaro, Susanna, the Count and Countess, Cherubino, Mar-
cellina and Bartolo are all characters brought fully to dramatic
life by musical means, and the twenty-minute-long finale to
Act II is often pointed to as a perfect example of the marriage
of music and drama in opera.

Don Giovanni (1787), dramatically less satisfactory
than *Figaro,* is in terms of musical characterisation perhaps an
even greater and more complex work, while *Così fan tutte*
(1790), an enchanting comedy, is in many ways closer to
perfection than either of the other two in its elegant formality
and musical wit.

In the final year of his life, Mozart composed two more
operas. *La Clemenza di Tito* (The Clemency of Titus) is a
return to the old *opera seria,* written for a royal occasion, while
Die Zauberflöte (The Magic Flute) is as much pantomime as
opera, a curious hybrid in which Mozart's deepest thoughts
about life and death, influenced by the Masonic society to
which he belonged, mingle with Viennese low comedy. *Die
Zauberflöte*, composed for the working-class audience of a
suburban Viennese theatre, is a unique work, confused,
inconsistent in style, and yet in its way sublime.

7

NINETEENTH CENTURY OPERA

If opera had been nothing but an aristocratic entertainment, it would not have survived the revolutionary spirit abroad in the nineteenth century. But it did survive, and it adapted itself to new and different audiences. Something of the spirit of the French Revolution is to be found in Mozart's *Le Nozze di Figaro* (though even more strongly in the Beaumarchais play on which the opera was based).

In France itself, the revolution certainly affected the opera of the time. The French *opéra comique* took a more serious turn, though the term itself continued to be used to differentiate an opera whose musical numbers were separated by spoken dialogue from one which was composed through-out. The leading French opera composers of the immediate post-revolution years were Méhul, Cherubini and Spontini, the latter two Italians who had established themselves in Paris. Méhul's most important work was *Joseph* (1807), based on the biblical story of Joseph and his brethren, an opera which is rarely performed today; Cherubini and Spontini, after years of neglect, are beginning to be performed again. Cherubini's *Medée* (1797) has the power and grandeur of the

French classical theatre translated into musical terms, and his *Les Deux Journées* (The Two Days: 1800) strongly influenced Beethoven when he came to write his only opera, *Fidelio*. Spontini's *La Vestale* (The Vestal Virgin: 1807) typifies in its stateliness the tastes and aspirations of the Empire period.

Fidelio

Beethoven's *Fidelio* (its first version, *Leonore*, appeared in 1805) was first produced at the Theater an der Wien in Vienna in 1814. It is the great composer's only opera, and there are some who claim it is not an opera at all, or at best a highly unsatisfactory one. It begins as domestic *opéra comique* and ends as romantic rescue opera, with elements of oratorio thrown in. Yet *Fidelio,* by virtue of its power and its humanity, transcends these categories. Some claim it to be the greatest opera written; it is certainly, in its celebration of the love of mankind, of conjugal love and fidelity, and of freedom, one of the most moving of operas and one of the masterpieces of the human spirit. *Fidelio* is not an easy work to stage: its truth can sometimes elude the most lavishly cast production and reside in a quite humble amateur performance. Given a reasonable level of musical accomplishment, sincerity will scale the heights of *Fidelio* more easily than will technique.

     Fidelio stands on its own and cannot be said to have influenced the course of German-language opera. The majority of operas staged in Vienna at the time of *Fidelio* were sung in Italian, and many of them were composed by Italians.

Cimarosa and Rossini

One of the most popular composers of Italian opera in Vienna at the end of the eighteenth century was Domenico Cimarosa, who for a time was Austria's Court Composer. Cimarosa's talent lay in the direction of comedy, though he also composed a number of serious operas. His most famous work, *Il Matrimonio segreto* (The Secret Marriage: 1792), was so successful at its first performance in Vienna that the Emperor Leopold II,

**Cimarosa
and
Rossini**

after having supper served to the cast, ordered the entire performance to be repeated.

The comic style of Cimarosa influenced a number of composers, not so much in Vienna where, in the early nineteenth century, a German-language opera was struggling to establish itself, but in Italy. The earliest operas of Gioacchino Rossini certainly owe a great deal to Cimarosa. Rossini, too, was temperamentally more suited to the creation of comedy than tragedy; of his nearly forty operas, the majority of the successful ones are *opere buffe,* comic operas. Rossini began his career with a one-act opera, *La Cambiale di matrimonio* (The Bill of Marriage), which was performed in Venice in 1810 when its composer was eighteen and which was successful enough to lead to several other commissions for one-act comic pieces.

Though his forte was comedy, Rossini's first important opera was his full-length *opera seria, Tancredi* (1813), based on a tragedy by Voltaire. Despite the uneven quality of its musical invention, *Tancredi* was highly acclaimed by its first audiences in Venice. One of its arias, 'Di tanti palpiti', a very catchy tune, became so popular that it was hummed and whistled in the streets and alleyways of Venice from morning till night. Three months after the premiere of *Tancredi,* Rossini scored an even greater success in Venice, this time with a comic opera, *L'Italiana in Algeri* (The Italian Girl in Algiers).

With *L'Italiana in Algeri,* an opera still popular with audiences today, Rossini found himself famous throughout Italy. His next real success came, not with comedy, but with the historical drama *Elisabetta, Regina d'Inghilterra* (Elizabeth, Queen of England: 1815). It was with this opera that Rossini began his practice of writing out fully the decorations and embellishments to his melodies that he was willing to accept, rather than leave them to the uncertain taste of his performers.

The opera which Rossini composed in less than a fortnight in 1815 for the Teatro Argentina in Rome is generally regarded today as being his masterpiece, and certainly one of the most popular operatic comedies in the repertoire: *Il Barbiere di Siviglia* (The Barber of Seville). One of the reasons that he was able to compose the work so quickly was that

Rossini was a great borrower from himself: most of his operas contain at least one number lifted from an earlier work. Some of the music of *The Barber of Seville* had already been heard in *Elisabetta*, but by far the greater part of the opera is original, and the quality of invention throughout is remarkably high. This engagingly high-spirited comic opera is as fresh to the ear today as when it first burst upon its Roman audience in 1816.

Cimarosa and Rossini

After *The Barber of Seville*, Rossini began to turn out operas in quick succession. *Otello* (1816), based on Shakespeare's *Othello*, contains much beautiful music, though it is lacking in dramatic impetus. *La Cenerentola* (Cinderella: 1817) may not be the equal of *The Barber of Seville*, but it is an entertaining work which is still frequently staged.

In 1824, Rossini moved to Paris where he produced French-language versions of some of his Italian operas and then tried his hand at French *opéra comique* with *Le Comte Ory* (Count Ory: 1828), an elegant and charming comedy. His most important and influential opera for Paris, however, was *Guillaume Tell* (1829), based on the German playwright Schiller's play about the Swiss patriot William Tell. A large-scale work of great originality and power, *Guillaume Tell* came to influence an entire generation of French composers. Curiously, Rossini wrote no more works for the stage after *Guillaume Tell*, although he was only thirty-seven and at the height of his creative powers. He lived on to the age of seventy-six, producing virtually no new music of any consequence.

the age of bel canto

Until the beginning of the nineteenth century, the development of opera throughout Europe had not thrown up any significant differences in national styles. But during the nineteenth century, as nationalism took a hold and as republican ideas advanced, a number of national differences in musical and operatic style began to emerge and the history of opera at this point begins to produce branch lines. Italian,

the age
of
bel canto

German, French and Russian opera, for instance, developed in ways which took them further apart from one another.

Italy embarked upon what has since become known as the age of *bel canto*, of beautiful singing. All operas, all songs, require beautiful singing, and to designate a particular period as that of *bel canto* is really meaningless. The operas of Handel and of Mozart certainly require to be sung beautifully. But Rossini and more especially his followers Bellini, Donizetti and, to a lesser and more complex extent, Verdi, wrote for the voice in such a way that dramatic expressiveness could be achieved through purely vocal means. The Italian language facilitated this, just as the German and English languages led to a different type of voice production and thus a different style of singing, and a different kind of music and of interpretation.

Bellini lacked the vivacity and humour of Rossini, and it could also be said that he lacked the earlier composer's command of the grand manner. His greatest asset was a gift for long, elegantly phrased elegiac melody. His delicate yet enduring tunes have much in common with the Nocturnes and Études of Chopin, a composer who was strongly influenced by Bellini's operas. Of the ten operas Bellini composed during his brief lifetime of thirty-four years, *Norma* (1831) is generally regarded as the finest and one of the great masterpieces of the *bel canto* era, but earlier works such as *La Sonnambula* (The Sleepwalker: 1831) with its rustic charm, and *Il Pirata* (The Pirate: 1827), more dramatically vigorous, are also attractive. With his final opera, *I Puritani* (The Puritans: 1835), it seemed as though Bellini was entering upon a transitional stage. His death, only months after its première, robbed the Italian lyric stage of a precocious genius. It is chastening to think that, had Bellini lived a normal span of years, the operas just mentioned would probably be thought of merely as his juvenilia.

The character of Donizetti's genius was quite different from that of Bellini, more extrovert and therefore more obviously dramatic. By the time of his death at the age of fifty, Donizetti had composed nearly seventy operas, having turned out dramas, comedies, historical or tragic pieces with equal facility. Opera in Italy was now the most popular form of

theatre, and composers were under intense pressure to produce new works each season. Donizetti was able to set words
to music almost more quickly than his librettists could supply
them, and in some years he composed as many as three or four
operas. In 1830, he composed five. He proved himself an all-
round composer, as willing to compose farce and *opera buffa*
as he was to provide those romantic operas, often on historical
subjects, which were enormously popular. Though he never
really relaxed his manic pace of composition, it is just possible
to discern that he took rather more care with the works he
wrote from 1832 onwards; the dividing line being his warm-
hearted and melodically generous romantic comedy, *L'Elisir
d'amore* (The Love Potion: 1832). Certainly the proportion of
successes to failures is higher after that year.

Today, three of Donizetti's comedies are still highly
popular. They are *L'Elisir d'amore, La Fille du régiment* (The
Daughter of the Regiment: 1840) and *Don Pasquale* (1843). Of
his tragedies, *Lucia di Lammermoor* (1835), Donizetti's
greatest success during his lifetime, has remained a popular
favourite. Other Donizetti operas disappeared from the stage
for many years, but have come back into favour in recent
years because a generation of singers capable of doing justice
to them began to appear on the scene: singers such as Maria
Callas, Joan Sutherland, Giulietta Simionato, Leyla Gencer,
Montserrat Caballé, Nicolai Gedda, Alfredo Kraus. Among
the most lively of Donizetti's serious operas which have
recently been revived are *Lucrezia Borgia* (1833), *La Favorite*
(The Favourite: 1840), *Anna Bolena* (1830) and *Maria Stuarda*
(1834).

Verdi

Italy's greatest composer, Giuseppe Verdi, spans the world of
nineteenth-century Italian opera like a colossus. His earliest
opera, *Oberto* (1839), was composed when he was in his mid-
twenties; his last, *Falstaff* (1893), was produced in his eightieth year – and the composer lived on for a further eight years.
Oberto contains elements of Donizetti and even Bellini in its

Verdi

vocal writing, but its elemental vigour and rhythmic energy are new, and are Verdian. Verdi's first great success was his third opera, *Nabucco* (1842), which established him as the natural successor to Bellini and Donizetti. For the next few years, until the masterpieces of his middle period, he was sometimes to turn out operas at the rate of two a year. Most of them are uneven, and some of them contain passages of music which look crude or even awkward in score though they usually sound absolutely right in performance. None are dull and all possess that vivid creative energy which is the young Verdi's most valuable attribute.

Many of these early Verdi operas are now finding their way back on to the stage after years of neglect: *I Lombardi* (The Lombards: 1843), *Giovanna d'Arco* (1845), *Attila* (1846), *Il Corsaro* (The Corsair: 1848) and *I Masnadieri* (The Robbers: 1847), for example. Some, like *Ernani* (1844) and Verdi's first Shakespeare opera, *Macbeth* (1847), are superb operas by any standard.

The most popular of Verdi's middle period operas are the three which he produced between 1851 and 1853: *Rigoletto, Il Trovatore* (The Troubador) and *La Traviata* (The Wayward Woman). All three are remarkable for their melodic richness, and the first and last are also superbly constructed dramatically. *Rigoletto,* a particularly resilient work, based on Victor Hugo's play *Le Roi s'amuse* (The King Amuses Himself), triumphantly survives poor productions and the vain foibles of musically illiterate singers. Conversely, it offers magnificent opportunities to the intelligent interpreter of its title-role, a role infused, as is the entire opera, with great humanity.

Il Trovatore's effects are broad and immediate. The wealth of melody, the almost brutal vigour and pace of the opera, are among the ingredients which have ensured its popularity since its first performance. The first performance of *La Traviata* was, however, a fiasco, and it was not until a new production was mounted with better singers the following year that the work was a success. Today it is so well-known amongst opera lovers, its melodies so much a part of their experience, that it is difficult to stand sufficiently far away from it to appraise it afresh. It is an opera in which all of Verdi's finest qualities are to be perceived: his technical

mastery, his humanity, his psychological penetration and his
unerring taste.

After *Un Ballo in maschera* (A Masked Ball: 1859),
Verdi's pace began to slow, and he produced only *La Forza
del destino* (The Force of Destiny: 1862) for St Petersburg and
Don Carlos (1867) for Paris before emerging from semi-
retirement with one of the grandest of all grand operas, *Aida*.
written for the Cairo Opera House and given its première
there in 1871. *Aida* is a remarkable work which has almost
become the victim of its own popularity. In a sense, it falls
between two styles, possessing neither the rough vigour of the
early works nor the maturity of the two Shakespeare operas
which were to follow it. In purely musical terms, however, it is
nothing less than a miracle of melodic beauty and imaginative
orchestration. Also, despite its two public scenes, it is the most
intimate of grand operas, and at its heart one senses Verdi's
own profound melancholy.

Otello (1887) is regarded by many as Verdi's finest
opera. It is certainly an incredibly fresh, youthfully inspired
score for a man in his seventies to have created. Verdi's
musical language and style are beyond praise, the melody as
glorious as in his younger days but now freed from the harmo-
nic strictures of that earlier period and able to range where it
will.

In his eightieth year, 1893, Verdi composed his final
opera, *Falstaff,* based on Shakespeare's *The Merry Wives of
Windsor. Falstaff* was given its première in Milan and again
the occasion was a triumphant success. There is so much to
admire in *Falstaff:* scoring of chamber-music delicacy allied to
a wide, Beethovenian range of orchestral expression, the
magical evocation of forest and fancy in the last scene, and the
fantastic energy and pace of the entire opera which seems to
last no longer than one sudden flash of inspiration.

German Romantic opera

It was in Germany in the nineteenth century that the Romantic
movement had its strongest influence on opera. The great

pioneer of German Romantic opera is Weber, whose *Der Frei-schütz* (The Freeshooter: 1821) is a landmark in the history of German music. In many ways, *Der Freischütz* is a somewhat primitive and poorly put-together work; its tunes derive in part from the Italian opera of the day (mainly Rossini) and in part from German folk-song, while its naive and confused libretto is undramatic and clearly the work of an amateur. But it was from the beginning a popular work, and remarkable for the delicacy and poetry of Weber's orchestral writing. It is the greater emphasis placed on the orchestra rather than on the voice that distinguishes German from Italian opera. Despite the brilliance of Rossini's writing for the orchestra in *The Barber of Seville,* an opera roughly contemporary with *Der Freischütz,* one could listen to it sung without any accompaniment at all and yet get a fair impression of its flavour. But a performance of *Der Freischütz* without the orchestra would leave its audience with no clear idea of the opera's quality.

Weber's other operas contain a great deal of extremely attractive music, but they are dramatically so flawed that they are rarely staged. *Euryanthe* (1823), with virtually continuous music and no dialogue, certainly influenced Wagner's *Lohengrin,* but *Oberon* (1826), which Weber composed to a libretto in English for Covent Garden, represents a step back to the old opera of musical numbers separated by dialogue.

Wagner

The great genius of nineteenth-century German opera was Richard Wagner. Throughout the greater part of Wagner's life, appreciation of his operas was dependent upon agreement with his theories: theories of music drama and of a total art work, theories of economics and of the superiority of Aryans over Jews. But the point to remember about Wagner was his genius as a composer, before which the confused absurdity of his political, philosophical and aesthetic theories pales into insignificance. Even his theories about the total art work (*Gesamtkunstwerk*), a fusion of the arts of poetry, drama, music and the other arts of the theatre, are nothing more than a restatement of the principles laid down by the group of intellectuals in Florence, the Camerata, who brought opera into existence at the beginning of the seventeenth century.

Wagner's own earliest operas, *Die Feen* (The Fairies: written in 1833 but not performed until after his death) and *Das Liebesverbot* (The Ban on Love: 1836), based loosely on Shakespeare's *Measure for Measure,* owe as much to Italian opera, to Bellini and Donizetti, as to his German predecessors.

Wagner always wrote his own libretti. Though they are poor both as poetry and as drama, the libretti of Wagner's operas are what the composer needed to bring forth his music, for he was temperamentally incapable of collaborating with a poet or dramatist of genius. His first opera to achieve any success, *Rienzi* (1842), is far too long, like most of Wagner's works, and very uneven in quality, though its best scenes reveal something of the power of his later operas. There is much in *Rienzi* of Meyerbeer, the German Jewish composer who was the rage of Paris when Wagner was attempting in vain to establish a reputation there.

The first of Wagner's operas in which his genius shines forth unencumbered is *Der fliegende Holländer* (The Flying Dutchman: 1843). This is his most concise work for the stage, and one of the finest operas to emerge from German romanticism. *Tannhäuser* (1845), an attempt to deal with the problems of sacred and profane love, is in general too slow and stately for its subject matter, but *Lohengrin* (1850), a much more interesting work, stands at the crossroads in Wagner's career. Romantic in its almost Pre-Raphaelite purity and its static, two-dimensional characterisation, *Lohengrin* also contrives to anticipate the direction Wagner was to take in his next work, *Tristan und Isolde,* by virtue of its delicate balance, though not yet complete fusion, of music and drama.

German romanticism reached its peak with *Tristan und Isolde* (1865), which is virtually one long love-duet, and in which the drama is portrayed not by the singers on the stage, nor even to any great extent by their voices, but by Wagner's orchestra. *Tristan* is an opera for orchestra, with incidental voices. The score's heavily sensuous quality and the ecstatic richness of the orchestration give the work a curious psychological strength. It is in this opera that Wagner discovered how

Wagner   to reach simultaneously his audience's conscious and subconscious responses.

In his next opera, *Die Meistersinger von Nürnberg*
(The Mastersingers of Nuremberg: 1868), Wagner turned
aside to extol the virtues of the bourgeoisie, virtues which he
had never attempted to emulate in his own life. He composed
a light comedy which was also a hymn to artistic compromise
with, in its final scene, an irrelevant aside appealing to the
baser aspects of nationalism. But, simultaneously with *Die
Meistersinger*, Wagner was already deeply involved in the
gestation and creation of his masterpiece, *Der Ring des Nibe-
lungen* (The Nibelung's Ring).

The Ring, four separate full-length operas, was first
performed in its entirety in 1876 at Bayreuth, in the theatre
which Wagner caused to be built for the performance of his
own works. The individual operas are *Rheingold, Die Walküre*
(The Valkyrie), *Siegfried* and *Götterdämmerung* (The Twilight of the Gods). For all its unevenness and disproportionate
length, *The Ring* is Wagner's most important work and also
the one on which most critical estimates of the composer are
based. Such are the scale and nature of the enterprise that it
can be interpreted in terms of sociology, political history,
psychology or moral philosophy.

In the years following *The Ring*, Wagner composed his
final opera, *Parsifal* (1883). He himself conceived it as a
sacred, Christian music-drama; others have described it as an
attempt to give aesthetic validity to his racial prejudice, or
even as a celebration of high-minded, ascetic homosexuality.
Whatever else it may be, *Parsifal* is a complex work of art,
though its sickly, fin-de-siècle religiosity may not be to everyone's taste.

After the death of Wagner there did not appear to be
an obvious successor. A number of composers succumbed to
Wagnerism and produced operas in the style of the master,
but none was of sufficient individuality to survive comparison.
The only opera of outstanding interest to appear in Germany
in the years immediately following Wagner's death was *Hän-
sel und Gretel* (1893) by Humperdinck, who had been one of
Wagner's musical assistants at Bayreuth. It was not until the
emergence of Richard Strauss that German opera found its

A scene from the English National Opera production of Wagner's
Siegfried with Alberto Remedios in the title role.

Benvenuto Cellini by Berlioz in the Royal Opera production,
with Nicolai Gedda as Cellini.

next great composer. Strauss had already achieved fame as a
composer of orchestral music before he turned his attention to
opera in 1894 with *Guntram.* It was not until his second opera,
Feuersnot (Fire Famine), in 1900 that it became clear his
future would lie in that field.

grand opera

During the nineteenth century the French developed *grand
opéra,* mainly through the example of Meyerbeer who, with
his large-scale, five-act epics which invariably contained
huge choruses and spectacular ballets, may not have invented
the genre but certainly developed and perfected it. Rossini's
Guillaume Tell (1829) is one of the finest early examples of
French *grand opéra,* followed by Meyerbeer's *Robert le
Diable* (Robert the Devil: 1831), *Les Huguenots* (1836) and *Le
Prophète* (1849).

   In the latter half of the century, French opera may not
have contributed much to the development of the art form but
it did produce a few highly popular works which are still to be
encountered regularly in the opera houses of today. Chief
among these are Gounod's *Faust* (1859), Bizet's *Carmen*
(1875), Saint-Saens' *Samson et Dalila,* and, of the more prob-
lematical operas of Berlioz, *Benvenuto Cellini* (1838) and *Les
Troyens* (The Trojans: 1856–58).

   Massenet was the most consistently successful composer of French opera in the late nineteenth-century and his
operas have in recent years been returning to favour after a
period of comparative neglect. The voluptuous sweetness of
his style, his melodic charm and elegant romanticism are
found at their best in *Manon* (1884) and *Werther* (1887), but
almost equally enjoyable are *Le Roi de Lahore* (The King of
Lahore: 1877), *Hérodiade* (1881) *Esclarmonde* (1889) and
Thaïs (1894). Another French opera which deserves to be
mentioned even in a brief survey is Charpentier's *Louise,*
staged in Paris in 1900 and still to be heard occasionally in
France (and on two excellent gramophone recordings) if nowhere else. *Louise,* which tells the story of a poor dressmaker

and her artist lover in Paris at the turn of the century, is an attractive and unusual work, worth seeking out.

opera in Russia

The emergence of nationalism in the nineteenth century brought with it a surge of national feeling in all of the art forms – in painting, in literature, in the theatre and in music. Opera was an obvious field for the expression of nationalist feeling, and in many countries it freed itself from Italian influence only with the rise of nationalism. This was most noticeable in the Eastern European countries, and nowhere more strongly than in Russia. The earliest Russian operas were Italian in language as well as in style, and many of them were, in fact, composed by Italians employed at the court of the tsars. When a popular opera by a Russian composer, Glinka's *A Life for the Tsar*, appeared in 1836, it was referred to sneeringly by the aristocracy as 'the music of coachmen' simply because it was sung in Russian and made use of Russian folk melodies. 'What does that matter, since the coachmen are better than their masters?' Glinka is said to have remarked.

Listened to today, Glinka's opera sounds like a Russian equivalent of a charming *bel canto* opera from early nineteenth-century Italy, but when it was composed the use of Russian and Polish folk-song must have seemed either daring or trivial, depending on the listener's political attitudes as much as on his musical tastes. Dramatically, Glinka's opera is weak, but musically it is important since it led to the possibility of a Russian-language opera, and showed the way to composers of greater stature than Glinka, composers of such diverse styles as Tchaikovsky, Mussorgsky and Rimsky-Korsakov.

It is still not generally realised in the West that Tchaikovsky, whose symphonies and concertos form part of our staple musical diet, also wrote ten operas. *Eugene Onegin* (1879), based on the novel in verse by Pushkin, has long been popular, and *The Queen of Spades* (1890), which also has its source in a Pushkin novel, is occasionally performed. But the other operas, most of which continue to be staged in the Soviet

Union today, contain some of Tchaikovsky's most dramatic
and tuneful music, especially *Mazeppa* (1884), *Iolanthe* (1892) and *The Maid of Orleans* (1881), based on a Russian adaptation of Schiller's Joan of Arc play. *Eugene Onegin* is, nevertheless, Tchaikovsky's operatic masterpiece and is a delicate, lyrical work which avoids the vehemence of the symphonies and even avoids the dramatic construction of the composer's other operas. Tchaikovsky actually described it not as an opera, but as 'lyrical scenes'.

National feeling is all-pervasive in the operas of Mussorgsky, whose *Boris Godunov* (1874) is still today regarded as almost the official 'national anthem' of Russian opera. *Khovanshchina,* (The Khovanski Affair) left unfinished when Mussorgsky died in 1881, and completed by Rimsky-Korsakov, is also still performed in the Soviet Union, though its slow-moving story of religious strife in seventeenth-century Russia has militated against its popularity in the West. Nor have the operas of Rimsky-Korsakov, with the exception of *The Golden Cockerel* (1909), found much favour outside Russia. Perhaps this is because, despite their exotic orchestral colouring, their fairy story plots are too remote from Western European culture, and because there is, finally, an essential monotony in Rimsky-Korsakov's music.

Among operas of more than local interest produced by the nationalist movement in countries outside Russia are the Polish opera *Halka* (1850) by Moniuszko and a number of Czechoslovakian works, chief among them Smetana's *The Bartered Bride* (1870) and Dvorak's *The Jacobin* (1889).

the realist school

In 1890, Mascagni's one-act opera, *Cavalleria Rusticana* (Rustic Chivalry), won a prize offered by a publisher and was produced in Milan. This short opera brought to its composer instant fame, which he was not able to sustain with later works. *Cavalleria Rusticana* was immediately successful due to its mixture of sex-and-violence and loud orchestration, and it has remained popular ever since. It is usually staged with another short opera, *Pagliacci* (Clowns: 1892) by Leoncavallo.

the
realist
school

Between them, *Cav. and Pag.*, as they are familiarly known to opera-lovers, initiated a new fashion in Italian opera, that of *verismo*. This is simply the Italian word for 'realism'. *Verismo* concentrated on sordid dramas of low-life, as though that were all there was to reality.

After *Cavalleria Rusticana*, Mascagni went on to write a dozen more operas, none of which has survived other than precariously, with the possible exception of the charming but musically and dramatically slight *L'Amico Fritz* (Friend Fritz: 1891). Nor did Leoncavallo, in his later operas, ever equal *Pagliacci*, the one opera on which his reputation now rests. Other briefly popular composers of *verismo* were Giordano and Zandonai, the former with his operas *Andrea Chenier* (1896) and *Fedora* (1898) which are still occasionally to be encountered on the stage, and the latter with *Francesca da Rimini* (1914), though this opera is rarely staged today.

The realist school was mainly confined to Italian opera. It flourished in Italy until the early years of the twentieth century but was never really popular in other parts of Europe, although Massenet wrote an effective piece of French *verismo* in *La Navarraise* (The Girl from Navarre: 1894).

Puccini

Puccini began his career as a composer of the realist school, which he soon outgrew. After two only mildly successful operas, his first real triumph was achieved with *Manon Lescaut* (1893), based on the same source as Massenet's highly popular *Manon* of 1884, a novel by the Abbé Prévost. With *Manon Lescaut*, it was clear that the successor to Verdi had at last been found. Puccini went on from success to success: the three operas which followed *Manon Lescaut* became his most popular, and today are among the most popular of all operas: *La Bohème* (Bohemian Life: 1896); *Tosca* (1900) and *Madama Butterfly* (1904).

None of Puccini's later works achieved quite the same degree of success as those three operas though *La Fanciulla del west* (1910: based on the play *The Girl of the Golden West* by David Belasco) has in recent years been successfully

revived. Pucini's final opera, *Turandot*, left unfinished at his
death in 1924 and completed by Franco Alfano, is probably
fourth in order of popularity after the central trio.

Puccini's gift for memorable melody, his skill in writing for the orchestra, his simple and accessible style, and his
mastery of stage effect, all combine to make him the finest
composer of Italian opera after Verdi.

operetta

It would be wrong not to include operetta, or the lighter type
of opera, in this survey of nineteenth-century opera. In
Vienna, operettas are played in repertory along with operas in
the opera houses: operettas by Johann Strauss (*Die
Fledermaus:* The Bat, and *Der Zigeunerbaron:* The Gypsy
Baron), Franz Lehár (*Die lustige Witwe:* The Merry Widow),
Kalman, Oscar Straus, Robert Stolz and others.

In France and elsewhere, the operettas of Offenbach
are highly regarded: works such as *Orphée aux enfers*
(Orpheus in the Underworld: 1858), *La belle Hélène* (Beautiful Helen: 1864) and *La vie Parisienne* (Parisian Life). In England the Savoy Operas, so-called because the majority of them
were first produced at the Savoy Theatre, London, maintain
an enduring popularity. These operettas with texts by W. S.
Gilbert and music by Sir Arthur Sullivan are the principal
English contribution to operetta: *The Pirates of Penzance,
Iolanthe, The Gondoliers, H.M.S. Pinafore,* and *The Mikado*
are the most often performed.

Operetta strongly influenced the composers of early
twentieth-century American musical comedy, composers such
as Kern, Berlin and Romberg.

8

OPERA IN THE TWENTIETH CENTURY

Opera in the twentieth century has pursued a variety of paths. With certain exceptions which are noted below, the most popular operas actually composed during this century were the creations of men who were essentially nineteenth-century composers, and whose styles had been formed well before the turn of the century: Puccini and Strauss.

The early operas of Richard Strauss can fairly be called Wagnerian, but it was not long before he had added to the rich Wagnerian orchestral writing a sensuous quality of his own, and a more graceful melodic line. Strauss was also concerned to ensure that the words he set to music were of the highest possible literary quality. After setting a shortened translation of Oscar Wilde's play, *Salome* (1905), and startling the musical establishment of his day with the violence of his orchestration as well as the morbid psychology of the subject, Strauss began a long and productive partnership with the distinguished Austrian poet and playwright Hugo von Hofmannsthal. Von Hofmannsthal wrote the libretti of the composer's next four operas and, after a gap, a further two.

The first of the Strauss-Hofmannsthal collaborations

was *Elektra* (1909), a twentieth-century equivalent of the classical Greek theatre, but the most enduringly popular has
proved to be the opera that followed. This was *Der Rosenkavalier* (The Cavalier of the Rose: 1911), an elegant, sump-
tuously scored comedy set in eighteenth-century Vienna.
Ariadne auf Naxos (Ariadne on Naxos) still holds the stage in
its second version of 1916, as does *Die Frau ohne Schatten*
(The Woman Without a Shadow: 1919), the opera which
Hofmannsthal regarded as their finest joint creation. The final
opera of the Strauss–Hofmannsthal partnership, which ended
only with the death of the poet, was another Viennese comedy, *Arabella* (1933).

The gap in the flow of Strauss–Hofmannsthal operas
was caused when the composer wrote a quasi-autobio-
graphical piece, *Intermezzo* (1924), to his own libretto. The
works he produced after Hofmannsthal's death were
relatively less successful, with the exception of his final work
for the stage, *Capriccio* (1942).

Modern, 'twentieth-century' operas, as distinct from
nineteenth-century operas composed in the twentieth century, soon began to emerge. The first modern opera is Debussy's *Pelléas et Mélisande,* which was written in 1902 as a reac-
tion against Wagner.

A composer whose genius was more suited to opera
than that of Debussy was Maurice Ravel. Ravel composed
only two one-act pieces for the stage: the brilliant and witty
L'Heure Espagnole (The Spanish Hour: 1907) and *L'Enfant et
les Sortilèges* (The bewitched child: 1925), based on a libretto
by Colette.

Three of the six composers who comprised the group
known as *Les Six* (Durey, Honegger, Auric, Milhaud, Ger-
maine Tailleferre and Poulenc) made notable contributions to
French opera. Darius Milhaud's most important opera was the
remarkable *Christophe Colomb* (1928). The talent of Francis
Poulenc displayed two distinct facets, both of them quintes-
sentially Gallic in wit and religiosity. The former quality is displayed in the engaging and popular *Les Mamelles de Tirésias*
(The Breasts of Tiresias: 1947), while the latter found its finest
flowering in the conservative and sentimental *Dialogue des
Carmélites* (Dialogue of the Carmelites: 1957), an opera about

a group of nuns martyred during the French Revolution. Poulenc's most successful opera, however, is probably the one-act *La Voix humaine* (The human voice: 1959), based on a monologue by Cocteau, a highly effective piece for solo soprano which calls for a singing-actress of distinction. The stage work by Arthur Honegger which seems most likely to retain a place in the international repertoire is *Jeanne d'Arc au Bûcher* (Joan of Arc at the Stake: 1938).

Italy no longer leads the world in opera. A number of elderly *verismo* composers continued to produce new works in a played-out style up until the Second World War, but the younger Italian composers, torn between the Italian vocal tradition and the essentially non-vocal twelve-tone methods of such composers as Berg and Schoenberg, tended to lose their way and their confidence. The most noteworthy Italian composers of modern times are Pizzetti, Malipiero and Dallapiccola. Pizzetti's *L'Assassino nella cattedrale* (1958), based on T. S. Eliot's play *Murder in the Cathedral* about the martyrdom of Thomas à Becket, has been performed frequently outside Italy since its première. The composer was in his late seventies when he wrote it, and the score possesses something of the calmness and inaction of old age, if not its serenity. Pizzetti's contemporary, Malipiero, wrote several operas in a variety of styles and was to some extent the victim of his own restless fertility. The most unusual of his works for the stage is *L'Orfeide* (The Orpheus Trilogy), a huge trilogy which was first staged in German translation in 1925.

The leading operatic composer of post-war Italy has been Luigi Dallapiccola. He has in some measure succeeded in effecting a marriage between the requirements of his particular technique and the basically lyrical style still necessary when writing for the human voice. *Volo di notte* (Night Flight: 1940), a one-act opera based on the novel by Saint-Exupéry, is one of the most strikingly individual works composed in Italy in the last half-century, and *Il Prigioniero* (The Prisoner: 1950) is really contemporary both in musical technique and subject matter, a moving comment on the ingenuities of man's inhumanity to man.

Germany and Austria have between them taken on in the twentieth century the role played by Italy in the

Top: The brothel scene in the Glyndebourne Festival Opera production
of *The Rake's Progress* by Stravinsky. The designer was David Hockney.
Below: The front curtain for the same production.

Peter Pears as Aschenbach with Robert Huguenin (Tadzio) and
Deanne Bergsma (The Polish Mother) in the first production of *Death
In Venice* by Benjamin Britten at The Maltings, Snape, in 1973.

nineteenth. Among a number of successful composers of opera, the names which stand out are those of Busoni (who was half-Italian), Pfitzner, Hindemith, Weill, Orff, Blacher, Liebermann, Henze, Schoenberg, Berg, Schreker, Krenek, Korngold, and Von Einem. Even in a brief survey, six of the operas they composed must be given individual mention: Busoni's *Doktor Faust* (1925) is a poetic and individual re-telling of the Faust legend; *Palestrina* (1917) is Pfitzner's mov-ing act of homage to a great composer of the sixteenth cen-tury; Kurt Weill's *Dreigroschenoper* (Threepenny Opera: 1928) and *Aufstieg und Fall der Stadt Mahagonny* (Rise and Fall of the City of Mahagonny: 1930), both written in col-laboration with the poet Brecht, brought a 'popular', bitter and sardonic tone to opera and carried it to a wider audience; Alban Berg's *Wozzeck* (1925), a powerful expressionist drama, is perhaps the greatest opera the century has yet produced, and Berg's *Lulu*, left unfinished when the composer died in 1935 but recently completed from his sketches and staged in full, is in purely musical terms an even finer work.

Russian opera in the twentieth century is dominated by three names: Prokofiev, Shostakovich and one of the great geniuses of the century, Igor Stravinsky, whose later works composed to English texts can hardly be considered other than international. Stravinsky's earliest opera, *The Night-ingale* (1914), reveals the influence of his teacher, Rimsky-Korsakov, but his later works are unique and original. *Oedi-pus Rex* (1927), composed as an oratorio, lends itself effec-tively to stage performances. Stravinsky's operatic master-piece is *The Rake's Progress* (1951), written to a libretto by the poet W. H. Auden in collaboration with Chester Kallman.

Prokofiev's achievement in opera is uneven, but his lyrical gift is seen at its finest in his most famous opera, *The Love of Three Oranges* (1919), a satirical fairy-tale, and in *The Fiery Angel* (written in the twenties but not staged until 1955), a fascinating study in religious hysteria. The vast *War and Peace* (1942), based on Tolstoy, is an exciting spectacle though not first-rate Prokofiev.

The Soviet Union's most distinguished composer, Shostakovich, composed two operas – *The Nose* (1930) and *Katerina Ismailova*. *The Nose* is a satirical expressionistic comedy, and *Katerina Ismailova* (originally called *The Lady Macbeth of Mtsensk District* when it was first staged in 1934) is an unsuccessful attempt to combine the sentimental and the satirical. For no very clear reason, *Katerina Ismailova* fell foul of Soviet musical censorship and was suppressed for several years. Stagings of the revised version since 1959 have failed to establish the opera internationally.

British and American opera

A feature of opera in the twentieth century has been the emergence of English-language opera as a force to be reckoned with. Just as British and American singers and conductors have established themselves on the European scene, so the composers have begun to find acceptance outside their own countries. The operas of Vaughan Williams, among them *Hugh the Drover* (1924), *Sir John in Love* (1929) and *Pilgrim's Progress* (1951), are of purely local concern, but those of Delius, such as *A Village Romeo and Juliet* (1907) and *Fennimore and Gerda* (1919), are of wider interest. However, it was not until the arrival on the opera scene of Benjamin Britten with *Peter Grimes* in 1945 that the renaissance of English opera finally got under way.

Britten is arguably the finest twentieth-century composer of opera, and certainly the greatest composer England has produced since Purcell. His genius for characterisation and for setting the English language, and his unerring dramatic sense, were displayed in a remarkable series of works for the stage. Some, like *Peter Grimes, Billy Budd* (1951) and *Gloriana* (1953), were scored for large orchestral forces, and some, including *The Rape of Lucretia* (1946), *Albert Herring* (1947), *The Turn of the Screw* (1954) and *A Midsummer Night's Dream* (1960), for smaller ensembles. *Owen Wingrave* (1971) was written for television and only later adapted for the stage. Britten's final opera, *Death in Venice* (1973), was based on the Thomas Mann novella of that title.

The great success of Britten was obviously an encouragement to two slightly older composers, William Walton and Michael Tippett. Walton's *Troilus and Cressida* was staged at Covent Garden in 1954 and revived some years later; Tippett's operas, musically more interesting than Walton's though married to somewhat obscure libretti of the composer's own devising, have included *A Midsummer Marriage* (1955), *King Priam* (1962), *The Knot Garden* (1970) and *The Ice-Break* (1977).

In recent years, a number of younger composers have had operas produced in Great Britain, among the most talented being Malcolm Williamson (Master of the Queen's Music), Nicholas Maw, Richard Rodney Bennett, Peter Maxwell Davies and Harrison Birtwistle.

There have been American operas of substance and stature since the middle of the last century, but it was not until the 1930s that a conscious attempt was made, by the Metropolitan Opera, to encourage native composers by commissioning and staging a number of works. Deems Taylor's *The King's Henchman* (1927) and his *Peter Ibbetson* (1931) were much acclaimed when they were first performed but they have not been revived. Neither Louis Gruenberg's *The Emperor Jones* (1933) nor Howard Hanson's *Merry Mount* (1934) has proved any more enduring. The Italian-American Gian Carlo Menotti began his career in 1937 with *Amelia al Ballo* (Amelia at the Ball), and went on to compose a series of light operas, somewhat Puccinian in idiom, the most successful of which were *The Medium* (1946) and *The Consul* (1950). Menotti has continued to compose operas, though his particular style of musical journalism appears to have gone out of favour.

Samuel Barber has composed two operas which were successfully staged: *Vanessa* (1958), at the old Metropolitan Opera, and *Antony and Cleopatra*, which opened the new Met in 1966. Both are agreeable and entertaining works, but more creative power and originality are to be found in Virgil Thomson's *Four Saints in Three Acts* (1934), its libretto by Gertrude Stein, and *The Mother of Us All* (1947), to another Gertrude Stein text. Aaron Copland's *The Tender Land* (1954) is more conventional in idiom, but no less enjoyable for that. Perhaps the most exhilarating American opera is George Gershwin's *Porgy and Bess* (1935), which was composed for a Negro cast.

For a time it seemed as though Leonard Bernstein

British
and
American
opera

might become an opera composer of importance. However, his *Trouble in Tahiti* (1952) was followed not by another opera but by a work for the Broadway musical stage, *West Side Story* (1957). It may well be that the Broadway musical is the real American equivalent of European opera. It is certainly true that Stephen Sondheim's *Sweeney Todd*, which played for about one hundred and fifty performances at London's Drury Lane Theatre in 1980, is a more valid and more enjoyable modern opera than any new work staged at the London opera houses with the exception of operas by Britten and Tippett.

The German Kurt Weill contributed works to Broadway, and such composers as Richard Rodgers *(Oklahoma, South Pacific, The King and I)* and Frederick Loewe *(My Fair Lady, Brigadoon, Camelot)* carried on the traditions of such earlier composers of American musical comedy as Jerome Kern *(Show Boat, Roberta)*, Victor Herbert *(Naughty Marietta)*, Irving Berlin *(Annie Get Your Gun, Call Me Madam)*, Rudolf Friml *(Rose Marie, The Vagabond King)* and Sigmund Romberg *(The Student Prince, The Desert Song)*.

9

THE
FUTURE
OF OPERA

In the second half of this century, opera, music and most other forms of art seem to have lost contact with their audience. Recently, however, there have been certain indications that composers are beginning to realise that, unless they can communicate with and can move an audience, their art will perish. Opera will not be kept alive by the acquisition of prizes and awards, or the acclamation of a small band of fellow-composers and critics. This is a problem which faces the arts in general, and opera in particular.

For today's audiences, is there not something wrong with an art form which would appear to have seen its best days in the past, which relies so heavily on revivals of eighteenth- and nineteenth-century works, and which is so expensive and cumbersome to stage? I do not think so. I am not sure that it is true that the masterpieces of opera are things of the past, and that opera is now a dead form. That assertion could be made, indeed is continually being made, about almost all kinds of art. We are constantly being told that the novel is dying, yet new novels – and very good ones – continue to appear. Where are the great painters and architects, people ask. For that matter, where are the poets to compare with Keats and Tennyson; where are the composers of symphonies to equal those of Beethoven and Brahms?

One of the answers is that the real geniuses in any form of art are always rare. A half-century separates Beethoven from Brahms, and Keats from Tennyson. We tend to telescope together the great figures of the past as though they lived in one glorious epoch. Opera today is as alive as the novel, the symphony, poetry, painting and architecture.

Composers of opera, like other artists, must experiment with the form, and not all experiments will be successful. The most interesting contemporary operas, however, are those which do build upon the experience of the past instead of rejecting it and attempting to start anew. Two of the most important composers of this century, Benjamin Britten (who died in 1976) and Michael Tippett, have written operas which are staged and re-staged, both here and abroad, because audiences find them enjoyable. Some younger composers, among them Peter Maxwell Davies and Harrison Birtwistle, want to take opera out of the opera house and into situations where it can be presented more simply – on the concert platform or in smaller halls with a minimum of staging. For that matter, Benjamin Britten, in addition to his operas written for conventional staging in opera houses and large theatres, also wrote short operas for performance in churches, which he called 'church parables'. Opera is alive today in a multiplicity of styles, and the great operas of the past are also alive, and accessible to anyone who will take the smallest amount of trouble to find out about them.

It is true that for the last three decades most art forms have been in a state of flux. Creativity has been at a relatively low ebb, as a quick glance at what is happening (and not happening) in painting, in poetry, in the theatre and in music will confirm. But there are signs that the arts are about to embark on a period of consolidation. If there is to be a future, all the arts will share in it, and our own era will, in retrospect, be seen to have played its part in their development. The opera of the future will be different from that of the past and, hopefully, superior to much of that of the present.

Punch and Judy by Harrison Birtwistle. In this 1982
Opera Factory London production at The Drill Hall, London, Punch
is sung by Omar Ebrahim and Judy by Hilary Western.

10

ONE HUNDRED OPERAS TO ENJOY

I have arbitrarily chosen one hundred interesting and enjoyable operas from among those which are most likely to be encountered in performance. They have all proved popular and enduring, and I have, in many cases, given an indication of their special appeal and highlights. I also recommend what seem to me to be the best recordings.

The operas are grouped under composers, and the listing of composers is chronological. Unless otherwise stated, the operas were originally written and performed in the language in which the title is listed.

I have not included the Gilbert and Sullivan operettas in my list, not because I do not think they deserve to be included, but merely because they are so accessible and so popular that they do not need to have anyone's attention especially drawn to them.

Opposite: Janet Baker in the title role in Gluck's *Alceste* at the Royal Opera House in 1982.

1   Purcell: *Dido and Aeneas*

Libretto by Nahum Tate, based on Book 4 of Virgil's *Aeneid;*
first produced at Josias Priest's School for Young
Gentlewomen, Chelsea, London, in 1689.

Dido, Queen of ancient Carthage, is made unhappy by her
love for Aeneas who, having fled from the sacking of Troy, is a
guest at her court. A sorceress and witches remind Aeneas of
his duty to travel on to Italy. Aeneas leaves, and Dido takes
her farewell of life in the famous lament, 'When I am laid in
earth', the best known number in the opera. She dies of grief,
and the opera ends with a chorus of mourning.

Recommended recording: Decca SOL 60047, with Janet
Baker (Dido), Raymond Herincx (Aeneas), conducted by
Anthony Lewis.

2   Pepusch: *The Beggar's Opera*

Libretto by John Gay; first produced at the Lincoln's Inn
Fields Theatre, London, in 1728.

A satirical play with music, about Macheath, a highwayman
whose downfall is brought about by his weakness for women
in general, and his involvement simultaneously with two
women in particular – Lucy, the daughter of a gaoler, and
Polly, the daughter of a 'fence'. A tragic end is averted by the
last-minute reprieve of Macheath as he is about to be hanged.

Modern performances are usually in arrangements either by
Frederic Austin (a version first given at the Lyric,
Hammersmith, London, in 1920) or Benjamin Britten (whose
edition was first performed at the Arts Theatre, Cambridge, in
1948). The many songs are tuneful and easy to remember. A
film version was made in 1953, with Laurence Olivier as
Macheath.

Recommended recording: Argo DPA 591–2, with Dennis
Noble (Macheath), Carmen Prietto (Polly), Martha Lipton
(Lucy), conducted by Richard Austin.

3   Handel: *Giulio Cesare*
        (Julius Caesar)

Libretto by Nicola Francesco Haym; first produced at the
King's Theatre, Haymarket, London, in 1724.

The opera, whose full title is 'Julius Caesar in Egypt', deals
with the relationship of Caesar and Cleopatra. After a number
of adventures and complicated intrigues, Caesar and
Cleopatra proclaim their love for each other, and Caesar has
Cleopatra crowned at Alexandria as Queen of Egypt. The
soprano arias for Cleopatra are among the highlights of the
opera.

Recommended recording: Deutsche Grammophon SLPM 138
637, excerpts consisting of arias for Caesar (Dietrich
Fischer-Dieskau) and Cleopatra (Irmgard Seefried),
conducted by Karl Böhm.

Among Handel's other forty or more operas are *Rinaldo,
Tamerlano, Rodelinda, Scipione, Alcina* and *Serse.*

4   Gluck: *Orfeo ed Euridice*
        (Orpheus and Eurydice)

Libretto by Ranieri Calzabigi; first produced at the
Burgtheater, Vienna, in 1762; revised version, in French, first
performed at the Opéra, Paris, in 1774.

The story is based on the classical legend of Orpheus who,
when his wife Eurydice dies, is offered by the gods the
opportunity to journey to Hades and bring her back, provided
that he does not look at her on the way. Orpheus manages to
soothe the furies and demons who confront him at the mouth
of Hades, and he enters the Elysian Fields where he finds
Eurydice. She, however, cannot understand why he will not
look at her, and fears he no longer loves her. He tries in vain to
comfort her, and at least turns to her and embraces her, at
which she falls dead. Orpheus sings his great aria of grief,

'Che faro senza Euridice?', and the gods again take pity on him. Eros appears, and restores Eurydice to life.

Recommended recordings: Italian version RCA SER 5539–41, with Shirley Verrett (Orpheus), Anna Moffo (Euridice), conducted by Renato Fasano; French version, World Record Club, OC 179–80, with Nicolai Gedda (Orpheus), Janine Micheau (Euridice), conducted by Louis de Froment.

Other operas by Gluck include *Alceste, Iphigénie en Aulide, Iphigénie en Tauride.*

5   Mozart: *Idomeneo, Rè di Creta*
(Idomeneus, King of Crete)

Libretto by Giambattista Varesco, based on an earlier libretto by Antoine Danchet; first produced at the Court Theatre, Munich, 1781.

Returning home after the Trojan war, Idomeneo is shipwrecked during a storm. He vows to sacrifice the first human he sees on shore, if the gods will save him. Reaching safety, the first person he meets is his son, Idamante. Idomeneo tries to evade his vow by sending Idamante away, but the island of Crete is ravaged by a monster, sent by the angry gods. Idamante, in love with Ilia, a captive Trojan princess, but loved by Electra, a Greek princess, fights and kills the monster, thus incurring the further wrath of the gods. Idomeneo is reluctantly about to sacrifice his son when Neptune intervenes, decreeing that Idomeneo shall abdicate and that Idamante shall rule in his place.

This is one of Mozart's finest operas, and it is historically important as an *opera seria* with a human face. But if you are approaching the Mozart operas for the first time, you would be wiser to start with *The Marriage of Figaro.*

Recommended recording: Philips 6703 024, with George Shirley (Idomeneo), Ryland Davies (Idamante), Margherita Rinaldi (Ilia), Pauline Tinsley (Electra), conducted by Colin Davis.

6   Mozart: *Die Entführung aus dem Serail*
     (The Abduction from the Harem)

Libretto by Gottlieb Stephanie Jnr., based on Christoph
Friedrich Bretzner's *Belmonte und Constanze;* first produced
at the Burgtheater, Vienna, in 1782.

Belmonte arrives at the palace of the Pasha Selim in Turkey,
seeking Constanze who has been captured along with her
maid Blonde and Belmonte's servant Pedrillo. The Pasha is in
love with Constanze, and his steward Osmin with Blonde, but
when Belmonte's plan for their escape fails, the Pasha
magnanimously gives them all their freedom.

The opera contains superb romantic arias for the soprano and
tenor roles of Constanze and Belmonte, and songs of comic
menace for the bass, Osmin. The Pasha Selim is a speaking
part only, and usually played not by a singer but by an actor.

Recommended recordings: Deutsche Grammophon 2740 102,
with Arleen Auger (Constanze), Peter Schreier (Belmonte),
Reri Grist (Blonde), Kurt Moll (Osmin), conducted by Karl
Böhm; performance in English on HMV SAN 201–3, with
Mattiwilda Dobbs (Constanze), Nicolai Gedda (Belmonte),
Jennifer Eddy (Blonde), Noel Mangin (Osmin), conducted by
Yehudi Menuhin.

7   Mozart: *Le Nozze di Figaro*
     (The Marriage of Figaro)

Libretto by Lorenzo da Ponte, based on the play *Le Mariage
de Figaro* by Beaumarchais; first produced at the Burgtheater,
Vienna, in 1786.

Figaro and Susanna, servants of the Count and Countess
Almaviva, are to be married, but the Count attempts to
postpone the ceremony for he hopes first to rob the girl of her
virginity. Through a series of complicated intrigues, Figaro
and Susanna manage to outwit the Count, who at the end of
the opera begs forgiveness of the Countess for his
philandering.

Among the best-known arias in the opera are Figaro's 'Non
più andrai', the Countess's 'Porgi amor' and 'Dove sono',
Susanna's 'Deh, vieni, non tardar', and the two songs sung by
the amorous page, Cherubino, 'Non so più cosa son' and 'Voi
che sapete'.

Le Nozze di Figaro makes a perfect introduction to the operas
of Mozart.

Recommended recording: Decca GOS 585–7, with Cesare
Siepi (Figaro), Hilde Gueden (Susanna), Alfred Poell (Count),
Lisa della Casa (Countess), conducted by Erich Kleiber.

8   Mozart: *Don Giovanni*

Libretto by Lorenzo da Ponte, based on several earlier
sources; first produced at the Nationaltheater, Prague, in
1787.

Don Giovanni, a notorious seducer of women, attempts to rape
Donna Anna, murders her father, and escapes. He and his
servant, Leporello, encounter one of Giovanni's former
mistresses, Donna Elvira, who prevents him from seducing a
peasant-maid, Zerlina. At a party at his villa, Giovanni is
unmasked by Donna Anna, her fiancé Don Ottavio and Donna
Elvira, but escapes. Eventually, he receives his just desserts
when a statue of Donna Anna's father comes to life, accepts
Giovanni's invitation to supper and arrives to drag him down
to hell.

Though this is a musically complex opera, much of its solo
music is simple and very easy to grasp at first hearing. Don
Giovanni's Serenade, for instance, and the duet, 'Là cì darem
la mano', in which he attempts to seduce Zerlina.

Recommended recordings: HMV SLS 5083, with Eberhard
Waechter (Don Giovanni), Joan Sutherland (Donna Anna),
Elisabeth Schwarzkopf (Donna Elvira), Luigi Alva (Don
Ottavio), Graziella Sciutti (Zerlina), Giuseppe Taddei
(Leporello), conducted by Carlo Maria Giulini; HMV SLS 923
172–5, with Nicolai Ghiaurov (Don Giovanni), Claire Watson

(Donna Anna), Christa Ludwig (Donna Elvira), Nicolai Gedda
(Don Ottavio), Mirelli Freni (Zerlina), Walter Berry
(Leporello), conducted by Otto Klemperer.

9 Mozart: *Così fan tutte*
(All women are like that)

Libretto by Lorenzo da Ponte: first produced at the
Burgtheater, Vienna, in 1790.

The opera is set in Naples in the eighteenth century where
two young officers, Guglielmo and Ferrando, wager their
cynical friend Don Alfonso that their respective lovers, the
sisters Fiordiligi and Dorabella, will remain faithful to them in
their absence. The men then pretend to go away to war, and
return disguised to attempt the seduction of each other's
fiancée. At first they are unsuccessful, but eventually the
sisters agree to marry the two strangers. At this point, the
strangers quickly disappear and the young officers return to
accuse Fiordiligi and Dorabella of infidelity. However, all
ends happily with a return to the *status quo*.

Fiordiligi's two great arias are superb showpieces for the
soprano.

Recommended recordings: HMV SLS 5028, with Elisabeth
Schwarzkopf (Fiordiligi), Christa Ludwig (Dorabella), Alfredo
Kraus (Ferrando), Giuseppe Taddei (Guglielmo), conducted
by Karl Böhm; Philips 6707 025, with Montserrat Caballé
(Fiordiligi), Janet Baker (Dorabella), Nicolai Gedda
(Ferrando), Wladimiro Ganzarolli (Guglielmo), conducted by
Colin Davis.

10 Mozart: *Die Zauberflöte*
(The Magic Flute)

Libretto by Emanuel Schikaneder, derived from a number of
sources; first produced at the Theater auf der Wieden, Vienna,
in 1791.

Tamino, saved from a serpent by three female attendants of
the Queen of Night, sets out with the birdcatcher Papageno to
rescue the Queen's daughter, Pamina, from the clutches of
Sarastro. In the course of his adventures, he discovers Sarastro
to be the embodiment of wisdom and truth, and the Queen of
Night to be motivated by evil. The opera ends with Tamino
successfully undergoing trials of his virtue and manliness, and
winning the hand of Pamina, while Sarastro and his followers
vanquish the Queen of Night.

The opera is a marvellous blend of the serious and the comic.
Papageno's songs have an engaging simplicity which anyone
can enjoy and appreciate.

Recommended recordings: HMV SLS 912, with Nicolai
Gedda (Tamino), Gundula Janowitz (Pamina), Lucia Popp
(Queen of Night), Walter Berry (Papageno), Gottlob Frick
(Sarastro), conducted by Otto Klemperer; historical recording
made in Berlin in 1937, on World Record Club SH 158–60,
with Helge Roswaenge (Tamino), Tiana Lemnitz (Pamina),
Erna Berger (Queen of Night), Gerhard Hüsch (Papageno),
Wilhelm Strienz (Sarastro), conducted by Sir Thomas
Beecham.

Other operas by Mozart include *La Clemenza di Tito, Lucio
Silla, La Finta giardiniera, Il Rè pastore.*

11   Beethoven: *Fidelio*

Libretto by Josef Sonnleithner, based on Bouilly's *Léonore, ou
L'Amour conjugal,* given its final form by George Friedrich
Treitschke; first produced, as *Leonore,* at the Theater an der
Wien, Vienna, in 1805; final version, *Fidelio,* produced at
Kärntnertor Theater, Vienna, in 1814.

Florestan, a Spanish nobleman, has been thrown into prison
by a political rival, Pizarro, the Governor of the prison.
Disguising herself as a youth, Florestan's wife, Leonore, takes
a job at the prison in the hope of rescuing her husband. Rocco,
the jailor, has a daughter, Marzelline, who falls in love with

Fidelio, the disguised Leonore. Leonore stops Pizarro from killing Florestan, and the arrival of a Minister of State leads to Florestan's release and the arrest of Pizarro. Among the highlights of the opera are the arias for Florestan and Leonore.

Recommended recording: HMV SLS 5006, with Christa Ludwig (Leonore), Jon Vickers (Florestan), Gottlob Frick (Rocco), Ingeborg Hallstein (Marzelline), conducted by Otto Klemperer.

12   Weber: *Der Freischütz*
(The Freeshooter)

Libretto by Friedrich Kind, based on a story in the *Gespensterbuch* (Ghostbook) of Johann Apel and Friedrich Laun; first produced at the Schauspielhaus, Berlin, in 1821.

The huntsman Max, in love with the head ranger's daughter, Agathe, is tricked by Kaspar into accepting magic bullets from the evil spirit Samiel, and thus winning a shooting contest and the hand of Agathe. Max almost kills Agathe under the spell of Samiel's evil, but all ends happily with Max's repentance and forgiveness, and his betrothal to Agathe. Max's aria is one of the great romantic highlights of German romantic opera.

Recommended recording: Deutsche Grammophon 2726 061, with Irmgard Seefried (Agathe), Richard Holm (Max), Kurt Boehme (Kaspar), conducted by Eugen Jochum.

Other operas by Weber include *Euryanthe* and *Oberon*.

13   Meyerbeer: *Les Huguenots*
(The Huguenots)

Libretto by Eugène Scribe; first produced at the Opéra, Paris, in 1836.

The opera uses the background of the 1572 Massacre of St. Bartholomew, when French Huguenots were slaughtered by

Catholics, to tell a fictional story involving Raoul de Nangis, a Huguenot nobleman, and his love for Valentine, the daughter of a leading Catholic. The events are too complex to be described briefly, but the climax of the opera is the massacre in which Raoul is killed.

The opera lends itself well to spectacular staging, but the individual characterization is more interesting than in most operas by Meyerbeer.

Recommended recording: Decca SET 460–3 with Martina Arroyo (Valentine), Anastasios Vrenios (Raoul), Joan Sutherland (Marguerite de Valois), conducted by Richard Bonynge.

14   Meyerbeer: *L'Africaine*
(The African Girl)

Libretto by Eugène Scribe; first produced at the Opéra, Paris, in 1865.

The naval officer Vasco da Gama sails to find a new land beyond Africa, but is wrecked on the African coast, and returns to Portugal with two captives, Selika and Nelusko. Selika, who is in love with Vasco, kills herself so that Vasco can return to his former love, Inez. Nelusko, in love with Selika, chooses death by her side.

Vasco da Gama's aria, 'O Paradis', is a great favourite with tenors, many of whom have recorded it in Italian as 'O Paradiso'.

Recommended recording: at present there is no commercial recording of *L'Africaine*. Through specialist dealers it is possible to obtain a recording taken from a performance at the San Francisco Opera in 1972, with Shirley Verrett (Selika) and Placido Domingo (Vasco da Gama), conducted by Michel Perisson (on Morgan Records 4 MOR 7202).

Other operas by Meyerbeer include *Le Prophète* and *Robert le Diable*.

15   Rossini: *L'Italiana in Algeri*
         (The Italian Girl in Algiers)

Libretto by Angelo Anelli; first produced at the Teatro San Benedetto, Venice, in 1813.

A comedy about a young Italian woman, Isabella, who in company with her elder admirer Taddeo is shipwrecked on the shores of Algiers, and brought before Mustapha, the Bey. There she finds her lover Lindoro whom she has been seeking, and who is a slave of the Bey. She finds a way to outwit Mustapha, and escape back to Italy with Lindoro, but not before persuading Mustapha to return to the wife he has been neglecting. The bubbling wit and tunefulness of Rossini's music makes this a highly enjoyable opera.

Recommended recording: Decca SET 262–4, with Teresa Berganza (Isabella), Luigi Alva (Lindoro), Rolando Panerai (Taddeo), Fernando Corena (Mustapha), conducted by Silvio Varviso.

16   Rossini: *Il Barbiere di Siviglia*
         (The Barber of Seville)

Libretto by Cesare Sterbini, based on the play, *Le Barbier de Séville* by Beaumarchais; first produced at the Teatro Argentina, Rome, in 1816.

Rossini's comic masterpiece, whose plot deals with the attempts of Count Almaviva to win the hand of Rosina and to thwart her guardian, Doctor Bartolo, who plans to marry her himself. Enlisting the aid of Figaro, the local barber and general factotum, Almaviva gains entrance into Bartolo's house by disguising himself first as a drunken soldier and then as an assistant of Basilio, Rosina's music teacher. The opera ends happily with the marriage of Rosina and Almaviva. (The adventures of Figaro with the Almavivas after their marriage were related in another play by Beaumarchais, *Le Mariage de*

Figaro, which is the basis of Mozart's opera, *Le Nozze di Figaro.*)

There can be few operas more tuneful and amusing than this. Figaro's entrance song, 'Largo al Factotum', is known to millions who have never seen the opera, for there can be few well-known baritones who have not recorded it.

Recommended recordings: HMV SLS 853, with Maria Callas (Rosina), Tito Gobbi (Figaro), Luigi Alva (Almaviva), Fritz Ollendorf (Bartolo), Nicola Zaccaria (Basilio), conducted by Alceo Galliera; HMV SLS 985, with Beverly Sills (Rosina), Sherrill Milnes (Figaro), Nicolai Gedda (Almaviva), Renato Capecchi (Bartolo), Ruggero Raimondi (Basilio), conducted by James Levine. The first of these two recordings omits Almaviva's aria in Act II, as do most recordings; but the second is complete.

17   Rossini: *La Cenerentola*
(Cinderella)

Libretto by Jacopo Ferretti, based on the fairy-tale by Charles Perrault; first produced at the Teatro Valle, Rome, in 1817.

The plot of *La Cenerentola* follows the outline of the Cinderella story, with the exception that the magical or supernatural element is missing. Cenerentola, whose real name is Angelina, is bullied by her father Don Magnifico and her step-sisters, who go to a ball at the palace without her. But Prince Ramiro, disguised as his valet Dandini, has already met Cenerentola and fallen in love with her. Alidoro, the Prince's tutor, helps her to get to the ball, and the familiar story moves to its happy conclusion. The best-known aria comes at the end of the opera, when Cenerentola sings of her happiness.

Recommended recording: Decca GOS 631–3, with Giulietta Simionato (Cenerentola), Ugo Benelli (Ramiro), Paolo Montarsolo (Don Magnifico), Giuseppe Foiani (Alidoro), conducted by Olivero de Fabritiis.

18   Rossini: *Guillaume Tell*
         (William Tell)

Libretto by Etienne de Jouy, Florent Bis, and Armand
Marrast, based on Schiller's play, *Wilhelm Tell*; first produced
at the Opéra, Paris, in 1829.

The opera follows the outline of Schiller's play, telling the
familiar story of William Tell, the thirteenth-century Swiss
patriot who rallied his countrymen against their Austrian
overlords. The incident in which the tyrant Gesler forces Tell
to shoot an apple from the head of his son Jemmy is included,
and a sub-plot deals with the love of another Swiss patriot,
Arnold, for the Austrian princess, Mathilde.

The overture is very well known as a concert piece and in
countless arrangements. Rossini's tunefulness is in plentiful
supply throughout the opera.

Recommended recording: HMV SLS 970, with Gabriel
Bacquier (Tell), Montserrat Caballé (Mathilde), Nicolai Gedda
(Arnold), Mady Mesplé (Jemmy), conducted by Lamberto
Gardelli.

Other operas by Rossini include *Elisabetta, Regina
d'Inghilterra, Armida, Mosé in Egitto, La Donna del lago, La
Gazza ladra, Semiramide* and *Le Comte Ory.*

19   Donizetti: *Anna Bolena*
         (Anne Boleyn)

Libretto by Felice Romani; first produced at the Teatro
Carcano, Milan, in 1830.

The opera is loosely based on history, telling the story of
Henry VIII's love for Jane Seymour, and his determination to
rid himself of his wife Anne Boleyn. Anne is falsely accused of
adultery with her former lover, Percy, Earl of
Northumberland, and condemned to death. The opera ends as
she goes to her execution, with an exciting aria and cabaletta.

Recommended recording: Decca SET 446–9, with Elena

Suliotis (Anna), Nicolai Ghiaurov (Henry VIII), Marilyn Horne
(Jane Seymour), John Alexander (Percy), conducted by Silvio
Varviso.

20   Donizetti: *L'Elisir d'amore*
(The Love Potion)

Libretto by Felice Romani, based on Scribe's libretto for
Auber's opera, *Le Philtre*; first produced at the Teatro della
Canobbiana, Milan, in 1832.

The young peasant Nemorino is in love with the wealthy
farm-owner, Adina, but finds courage to approach her only
when he has drunk what purports to be a love potion sold to
him by the quack Dulcamara. As it is merely cheap claret, it
has no effect, and Nemorino almost loses Adina to Sergeant
Belcore. However, after a number of complications, Adina
declares her love for Nemorino.

The opera contains one of the most beautiful of all tenor arias,
'Una furtiva lagrima', and the entire score is one of the
masterpieces of the *bel canto* era.

Recommended recordings: Decca GOS 566–7, with Hilde
Gueden (Adina), Giuseppe di Stefano (Nemorino), Renato
Capecchi (Belcore), Fernando Corena (Dulcamara),
conducted by Francesco Molinari-Pradelli; HMV SLS 925,
with Mirella Freni (Adina), Nicolai Gedda (Nemorino), Mario
Sereni (Belcore), Renato Capecchi (Dulcamara), conducted by
Francesco Molinari-Pradelli.

21   Donizetti: *Lucrezia Borgia*

Libretto by Felice Romani, based on the play *Lucrèce Borgia*
by Victor Hugo; first produced at La Scala, Milan, in 1833.

Lucrezia Borgia's husband, Alfonso, Duke of Ferrara, suspects
her of having an affair with a young man who is, in fact, her

son, Gennaro, though only she knows it. When she poisons a number of her enemies, Lucrezia is appalled to find Gennaro amongst them. He learns of their relationship just as he dies, and Lucrezia, overcome with grief, falls lifeless upon his body.

This is one of Donizetti's most dramatic works, but is no less tuneful than his comedies or romantic operas.

Recommended recording: Decca D93D3, with Joan Sutherland (Lucrezia), Giacomo Aragall (Gennaro), Ingvar Wixell (Alfonso), conducted by Richard Bonynge.

22 Donizetti: *Lucia di Lammermoor*

Libretto by Salvatore Cammarano, based on Sir Walter Scott's novel, *The Bride of Lammermoor;* first produced at the Teatro San Carlo, Naples, in 1835.

Motivated by greed, Henry Ashton (Enrico) tricks his sister Lucy (Lucia) into rejecting Edgar (Edgardo) whom she loves, and marrying Arthur (Arturo). When Edgar interrupts the wedding celebrations, and curses Lucy for her lack of faith, she loses her mind. On her wedding night, she stabs her husband. Her subsequent mad scene is one of the most famous in opera, and has been recorded by countless sopranos. Lucy dies, and Edgar, in despair, kills himself.

In addition to the Mad Scene, a famous highlight of the opera is the Sextet which occurs during the scene of Lucy's wedding. It is, in fact, one of the best-known tunes in all opera.

Recommended recordings: Decca SET 528–30, with Joan Sutherland (Lucia), Luciano Pavarotti (Edgardo), Sherrill Milnes (Enrico), conducted by Richard Bonynge; HMV SLS 5056, with Maria Callas (Lucia), Giuseppe di Stefano (Edgardo), Tito Gobbi (Enrico), conducted by Tullio Serafin.

23   Donizetti: *La Fille du régiment*
(The Daughter of the Regiment)

Libretto by Vernoy de Saint-Georges and Bayard; first
produced at the Opéra-Comique, Paris, in 1840.

Marie has been brought up in a Tyrolean village by a
regiment of soldiers and their Sergeant, Sulpice. She is in love
with Tonio, a local youth, and is distressed when it is
discovered that she is the niece of a Marquise, and is forced to
go and live with her relative. Tonio and the regiment manage
to find their way to her, the Marquise is discovered to be
Marie's mother, and gives her blessing to the marriage of
Marie and Tonio.

One of Donizetti's most charming and tuneful works, the
opera is often sung in Italian as *La Figlia del Reggimento:*

Recommended recording: Decca SET 372–3, with Joan
Sutherland (Marie), Luciano Pavarotti (Tonio), Spiro Malas
(Sulpice), Monica Sinclair (Marquise), conducted by Richard
Bonynge.

24   Donizetti: *Don Pasquale*

Libretto by Giovanni Ruffini and the composer, after Anelli's
libretto for an earlier opera, *Ser Marc' Antonio* by Pavesi; first
produced at the Théâtre-Italien, Paris, in 1843.

Don Pasquale, a rich old bachelor, has decided to marry and
thus deprive his nephew Ernesto of his inheritance, since he
disapproves of Ernesto's intended bride, Norina. Norina,
Ernesto and Pasquale's friend, Doctor Malatesta, trick the old
man into a false marriage ceremony with the gentle Sofronia,
who is really Norina heavily veiled, and who becomes
positively shrewish immediately after the ceremony.
Eventually, the 'marriage' is annulled, and Pasquale agrees to
the union of Norina and Ernesto.

Recommended recording: Decca SET 280–1, with Graziella

Sciutti (Norina), Fernando Corena (Don Pasquale), Juan
Oncina (Ernesto), Tom Krause (Malatesta), conducted by
Istvan Kertesz.

Other operas by Donizetti include *Roberto Devereux, La
Favorite, Linda di Chamounix, Maria Stuarda.*

25   Bellini: *La Sonnambula*
(The Sleep-walker)

Libretto by Felice Romani; first produced at the Teatro
Carcano, Milan, in 1831.

In a Swiss village, Amina, whose mother is the owner of the
local mill, is betrothed to Elvino, a young farmer. When Count
Rodolfo returns to the village after an absence of many years,
he stays at the inn. A scandal ensues when Amina is
discovered asleep in the Count's room at night, but all ends
happily when it is proved that Amina is a sleep-walker. (At
the climax of the opera, she is seen perilously walking in her
sleep across an insecure bridge over the mill-stream.) Bellini's
long sinuous melodies are very beautiful, and the opera's air
of pastoral charm is especially attractive.

Recommended recording: Decca SET 239–41 with Joan
Sutherland (Amina), Nicola Monti (Elvino), Fernando Corena
(Rodolfo), conducted by Richard Bonynge.

26   Bellini: *Norma*

Libretto by Felice Romani, based on the play *Norma* by
Alexandre Soumet; first produced at La Scala, Milan, in 1831.

When Norma, a Druid priestess in Gaul in Roman times,
discovers that her secret lover, Pollione, a Roman pro-consul
by whom she has had two children, has now transferred his
affections to a younger priestess, Adalgisa, she vows revenge.
Eventually, Norma denounces Pollione but also confesses her

own crime, and is condemned to die with him. Norma's aria,
'Casta diva', is one of the great showpieces of *bel canto*, and a
severe test for the soprano.

Recommended recordings: HMV ASD 3626–28, with Maria
Callas (Norma), Christa Ludwig (Adalgisa), Franco Corelli
(Pollione), conducted by Tullio Serafin; Decca SET 424–6,
with Joan Sutherland (Norma), Marilyn Horne (Adalgisa),
John Alexander (Pollione), conducted by Richard Bonynge.

27   Bellini: *I Puritani*
(The Puritans)

Libretto by Carlo Pepoli, based on the play *Têtes Rondes et
Cavaliers* by Ancelot and Saintine; first produced at the
Théâtre-Italien, Paris, in 1835.

The opera is set in Plymouth in the middle of the seventeenth
century, during the English Civil War. Elvira, daughter of the
Puritan Lord Walton, is about to marry the Cavalier Arturo,
when Arturo helps Henrietta, widow of Charles I, to escape,
and is forced to flee. Elvira, thinking she has been betrayed by
Arturo, loses her reason, which is restored at the end of the
opera when she is reunited with Arturo who has been
pardoned by Cromwell, now Lord Protector of the country.
Elvira's music is both tuneful and exciting. The tenor, Arturo,
is required to sing up to a high D in full voice, and even to the
F above in 'mixed voice' or supported falsetto.

Recommended recordings: ABC Records ATS 20016, with
Beverly Sills (Elvira), Nicolai Gedda (Arturo), Louis Quilico
(Riccardo), conducted by Julius Rudel; Decca SET 259–61,
with Joan Sutherland (Elvira), Luciano Pavarotti (Arturo),
Piero Cappuccilli (Riccardo), conducted by Richard Bonynge.

Other operas by Bellini include *Beatrice di Tenda, I Capuleti
ed i Montecchi, Il Pirata.*

28   Berlioz: *Benvenuto Cellini*

Libretto by Léon de Wailly and August Barbier, based on
Benvenuto Cellini's Memoirs; first produced at the Opéra,
Paris, in 1838.

Cellini plans to elope with Teresa during the Roman Carnival,
but in the confusion of the Carnival he is involved in a brawl
and kills a man. He is to be arrested for murder unless he
finishes by midnight a statue commissioned by the Pope.
Despite the machinations of Fieramosca, his rival in art and in
love, Cellini succeeds in casting his Perseus and obtaining a
pardon. The music for the Roman Carnival is well known
outside opera, and the tenor arias for Cellini are among
Berlioz's finest.

Recommended recording: Philips 6707 019, with Nicolai
Gedda (Cellini), Christiane Eda-Pierre (Teresa), Robert
Massard (Fieramosca), conducted by Colin Davis.

29   Berlioz: *Les Troyens*
                   (The Trojans)

Libretto by the composer, after Virgil's *Aeneid*; first produced
in Karlsruhe, Germany, in 1890. (Berlioz had agreed in 1863 to
divide the five-act opera into two parts, with Acts I and II as
Part One, *La Prise de Troie* (The Capture of Troy), and the
remaining three acts as Part Two, *Les Troyens à Carthage*
(The Trojans at Carthage). The latter part was performed in
Paris in 1863, but the complete work was not staged until
1890, when it was given on two consecutive nights.)

Part One deals with the episode of the wooden horse at Troy,
and the sacking of the city by the Greeks. Part Two tells the
story of Dido and Aeneas, ending with the suicide of Dido.

Les Troyens is one of the masterpieces of French opera, but it
is not the easiest of works for a novice to approach, because of
its length and complexity.

Recommended recording: Philips 6709 002, with Jon Vickers (Aeneas), Josephine Veasey (Dido), Berit Lindholm (Cassandra), conducted by Colin Davis.

30 Wagner: *Der fliegende Holländer*
(The Flying Dutchman)

Libretto by the composer, based on an episode in Heine's *Aus den Memoiren des Herren von Schnabelewopski*; first produced at the Hofoper, Dresden in 1843.

Condemned to sail the seas for ever, for having invoked the Devil's aid when rounding the Cape of Good Hope in a storm, the Dutchman is allowed ashore once every seven years. If he can find a woman who will be true to him, he will find redemption. Senta, daughter of the sea captain Daland, offers herself to him, but when he hears her in conversation with her former fiancé, Erik, the Dutchman feels himself betrayed. He sets sail again, Senta leaps into the sea after him, and he is redeemed by her love and faith.

One of Wagner's shortest operas, this is also one of his most immediately enjoyable. The spinning chorus and sailors' dance are well known.

Recommended recordings: RCA 2BB 109–11, with George London (Dutchman), Leonie Rysanek (Senta), Giorgio Tozzi (Daland), Karl Liebl (Erik), conducted by Antal Dorati; HMV SLS 934, with Theo Adam (Dutchman), Anja Silja (Senta), Martti Talvela (Daland), Ernst Kozub (Erik), conducted by Otto Klemperer.

31 Wagner: *Tannhäuser*

Libretto by the composer; first produced at the Hofoper, Dresden, in 1845.

The action takes place in mediaeval Germany. Tiring of the life of pleasure and lust he has been leading with Venus, the

knight Tannhäuser returns to his former life, and to Elisabeth
who loves him, and takes part in a song contest on the theme
of love. Wolfram and the other knights sing of courtly love,
which provokes Tannhäuser into singing the praises of Venus.
He is banished, to seek absolution from Rome, and when he
returns unsuccessful it is to find Elisabeth dead. As
Tannhäuser, too, falls lifeless, it is revealed that his soul has,
after all, been redeemed and forgiven.

Though slow-moving, this is one of Wagner's most enjoyable
operas. The Pilgrims' Chorus is well known out of context.

Recommended recording: HMV SLS 775, with Hans Hopf
(Tannhäuser), Elisabeth Grümmer (Elisabeth), Marianne
Schech (Venus), Dietrich Fischer-Dieskau (Wolfram),
conducted by Franz Konwitschny.

32   Wagner: *Lohengrin*

Libretto by the composer; first produced at the Hoftheater,
Weimar, in 1850.

When Elsa, in tenth-century Brabant, is accused by
Telramund of the murder of her brother, the mysterious
knight Lohengrin arrives to defend her. He offers Elsa his
hand in marriage on condition that she will never ask his
name or his origin. Telramund and his wife Ortrud sow seeds
of doubt and suspicion in Elsa's mind, and she breaks her
promise. Lohengrin announces that he had been sent by the
Holy Grail, and must now return whence he had come. Elsa
falls lifeless to the ground, as Lohengrin restores her
bewitched brother to her before departing.

This hypnotically powerful opera contains the Bridal March
used for weddings and known familiarly as 'Here comes the
bride!'

Recommended recording: HMV SLS 5071, with Jess Thomas
(Lohengrin), Elisabeth Grümmer (Elsa), Dietrich
Fischer-Dieskau (Telramund), Christa Ludwig (Ortrud),
conducted by Rudolf Kempe.

33   Wagner: *Tristan und Isolde*
        (Tristan and Isolde)

Libretto by the composer, based on the old Cornish legend;
first produced at the Hoftheater, Munich, in 1865.

The Cornish knight Tristan is bearing the Irish princess Isolde
to Cornwall to be the bride of King Mark. Isolde orders her
serving-maid Brangaene to prepare a death potion for her to
administer to Tristan and herself, but Brangaene substitutes a
love potion. As they are about to land, Tristan and Isolde drink
and confess their love for each other. Tristan attempts no
explanation when Mark surprises them together. He is
wounded by Melot, one of the King's followers, and taken to
Brittany to recover by his henchman Kurwenal. Isolde follows
Tristan to Brittany, but arrives just as he dies. She sings of the
fulfilment of their love in the realms of night and death, and
dies by Tristan's side. The climax of the opera, Isolde's
Liebestod, is the high peak of the romantic movement in
opera. *Tristan und Isolde* is Wagner's masterpiece.

Recommended recordings: HMV SLS 963, with Jon Vickers
(Tristan), Helga Dernesch (Isolde), Christa Ludwig
(Brangaene), Walter Berry (Kurwenal), conducted by Herbert
von Karajan; historical recording, made in 1952 on HMV RLS
684, with Ludwig Suthaus (Tristan), Kirsten Flagstad (Isolde),
Blanche Thebom (Brangaene), Dietrich Fischer-Dieskau
(Kurwenal), conducted by Wilhelm Furtwängler.

34   Wagner: *Die Meistersinger von Nürnberg*
        (The Mastersingers of Nuremberg)

Libretto by the composer; first produced at the Hoftheater,
Munich, 1868.

The action takes place in sixteenth-century Nuremberg, and
concerns the efforts of the cobbler-poet, Hans Sachs, to help
the young knight Walther von Stolzing achieve election to the

guild when Sachs persuades him of the wisdom of building upon tradition rather than rejecting it. In a stirring address to the crowd of citizens, Sachs preaches the virtue of honouring German art.

Walther's Prize Song is a popular aria, but the newcomer to opera should be warned that this comedy is very long and slow-moving.

Recommended recording: HMV SLS 957, with Theo Adam (Hans Sachs), Helen Donath (Eva), René Kollo (Walther von Stolzing), Geraint Evans (Beckmesser), conducted by Herbert von Karajan.

35 to 38   Wagner: *Der Ring des Nibelungen*
(The Nibelung's Ring)

A tetralogy of music dramas, with libretto by the composer, based on the old Nibelung Saga; first produced in its entirety at the Festival Theatre, Bayreuth, in 1876. The tetralogy consists of:

35   *Das Rheingold* (Rhinegold)

36   *Die Walküre* (The Valkyrie)

37   *Siegfried*

38   *Götterdämmerung* (The Twilight of the Gods)

The four operas trace the consequences of the theft of the Rhinegold from the river, first by the dwarf Alberich who forges a magic ring from it, and then its theft from Alberich by the god Wotan. The curse placed by Alberich on all who strive for possession of the ring is finally lifted by the return of the ring to the element of water from which it came. (The story is too long and complicated to be told in synopsis form in these pages: the reader is referred to one of the excellent books on Wagner, mentioned in the section on further reading (pages 156 to 157).

The Ring is an important landmark in the history of opera, but it is not for all tastes. Those of northern rather than Latin temperament will derive most enjoyment from it. Almost everyone already knows the Ride of the Valkyrie from *Die Walküre.*

Recommended recording of the complete *Ring:* Deutsche Grammophon, with Thomas Stewart, Régine Crespin, Gundula Janowitz, Jon Vickers, Jess Thomas, conducted by Herbert von Karajan; Philips, with Theo Adam, Birgit Nilsson, Leonie Rysanek, James King, Wolfgang Windgassen, conducted by Karl Boehm; in English on HMV with Norman Bailey, Rita Hunter, Margaret Curphey, Alberto Remedios, conducted by Reginald Goodall.

39 Wagner: *Parsifal*

Libretto by the composer; first produced at the Festival Theatre, Bayreuth, in 1882.

The story is based on the legend of the Holy Grail, which is guarded by a band of knights in a castle in Spain in the Middle Ages. An elderly knight, Gurnemanz, attempts to help an unknown youth, Parsifal, to understand the mysteries of the Grail. But it is only when Parsifal visits the magic garden of Klingsor, and is kissed by Kundry, that he realises its significance and the meaning of the wound suffered by Amfortas, leader of the knights of the Grail. In the last act of the opera, Parsifal is able to heal Amfortas' wound and consecrate himself to the service of the Grail.

Wagner's last opera, *Parsifal* is his most solemn and Germanic.

Recommended recording: Philips 6747 250, with Jess Thomas (Parsifal), George London (Amfortas), Hans Hotter (Gurnemanz), Irene Dalis (Kundry), conducted by Hans Knappertsbusch.

40   Verdi: *Nabucco*

Libretto by Temistocle Solera, based on the play
Nabucodonosor by Anicet-Bourgeois and Francis Cornue;
first produced at La Scala, Milan, in 1842.

The opera's fictional plot is embedded in the Old Testament
story of King Nebuchadnezzar (Nabucco), and the captive
Hebrews in Babylon. Nabucco is overthrown by his daughter
Abigaille, but regains his sanity and his throne, and embraces
the Hebrew faith. Zaccaria, the High Priest of the Hebrews,
plays an important role in the opera, and the captives' chorus,
'Va, pensiero', one of the most affecting passages in the score,
was taken up by Verdi's audiences as a rallying cry against
Austrian occupation of northern Italy.

Recommended recording: Decca SET 298–300, with Tito
Gobbi (Nabucco), Elena Suliotis (Abigaille), Carlo Cava
(Zaccaria), conducted by Lamberto Gardelli.

41   Verdi: *Ernani*

Libretto by Francesco Maria Piave, based on the play *Hernani*
by Victor Hugo; first produced at the Teatro La Fenice,
Venice, in 1844.

The opera is set in Spain, in the early sixteenth century.
Elvira, about to be married to her elderly kinsman Don Ruy
Gomez de Silva, is in love with the bandit Ernani, who is really
a nobleman. Elvira is also loved by the King, Don Carlo, who
is about to be crowned Holy Roman Emperor. Ernani and
Silva join together to rescue Elvira when she is abducted by
Don Carlo, but at the end of the opera Ernani is forced by Silva
to repay a debt of honour by committing suicide.

Verdi's use of melody to enhance and forward the drama is
masterly. Some of the tunes may sound like the Salvation
Army, but they are none the worse for that.

Recommended recording: RCA SER 5572–4, with Carlo
Bergonzi (Ernani), Leontyne Price (Elvira), Mario Sereni (Don
Carlo), Ezio Flagello (Silva), conducted by Thomas Schippers.

42   Verdi: *Macbeth*

Libretto by Francesco Maria Piave, based on the play
Macbeth by Shakespeare; first produced at the Teatro della
Pergola, Florence, 1847.

The play follows the plot of Shakespeare's play quite closely,
though a number of scenes are truncated, and characters of
lesser importance omitted. Shakespeare's three witches have
become an entire chorus.

Recommended recordings: RCA VIC 6121, with Leonard
Warren (Macbeth), Leonie Rysanek (Lady Macbeth), Carlo
Bergonzi (MacDuff), Jerome Hines (Banquo), conducted by
Erich Leinsdorf; HMV SLS 992, with Sherrill Milnes
(Macbeth), Fiorenza Cossotto (Lady Macbeth), José Carreras
(MacDuff), Ruggero Raimondi (Banquo), conducted by
Riccardo Muti.

43   Verdi: *Luisa Miller*

Libretto by Salvatore Cammarano, based on the play *Kabale
und Liebe* by Schiller; first produced at the Teatro San Carlo,
Naples, in 1849.

Set in the Tyrol in the early seventeenth century, the opera
tells a story of love and intrigue. Luisa, daughter of a retired
soldier, is in love with Rodolfo, son of Count Walter. When
Rodolfo refuses to give up Luisa, the Count has the girl's
father arrested, and his henchman, Wurm, forces Luisa to
write a letter to Rodolfo, telling him that she is in love with

someone else. Rodolfo, thinking she has betrayed him, poisons himself and Luisa, but, learning the truth from her as they are dying, manages to kill Wurm. This opera contains one of Verdi's most beautiful tenor arias, 'Quando le sere'.

Recommended recordings: RCA SER 5713–5, with Anna Moffo (Luisa), Carlo Bergonzi (Rodolfo), Cornell MacNeil (Miller), Giorgio Tozzi (Count Walter), Ezio Flagello (Wurm), conducted by Fausto Cleva; Deutsche Grammophon 2709 096, with Katia Ricciarelli (Luisa), Placido Domingo (Rodolfo), Renato Bruson (Miller), Gwynne Howell (Count Walter), Wladimiro Ganzarolli (Wurm), conducted by Lorin Maazel.

44   Verdi: *Rigoletto*

Libretto by Francesco Maria Piave, based on the play *Le Roi s'amuse* by Victor Hugo; first produced at the Teatro La Fenice, Venice, in 1851.

Rigoletto, hunchback jester to the Duke of Mantua, has a daughter, Gilda, to whom the licentious Duke has been paying court in disguise. When Gilda is abducted and seduced by the Duke, Rigoletto arranges to have his master killed by Sparafucile, a professional assassin. Overhearing the plot, Gilda sacrifices her life for the Duke whom she loves.

Two of Italian opera's most famous pieces are to be found in *Rigoletto:* the Quartet, and the tenor aria, 'La donna è mobile'.

Recommended recordings: HMV ALP 1004–6, with Leonard Warren (Rigoletto), Erna Berger (Gilda), Jan Peerce (Duke), Italo Tajo (Sparafucile), conducted by Renato Cellini; HMV SLS 5018, with Tito Gobbi (Rigoletto), Maria Callas (Gilda), Giuseppe di Stefano (Duke), Nicola Zaccaria (Sparafucile), conducted by Tullio Serafin; Decca SET 542–4, with Sherrill Milnes (Rigoletto), Joan Sutherland (Gilda), Luciano Pavarotti (Duke), Martti Talvela (Sparafucile), conducted by Richard Bonynge.

45   Verdi: *Il Trovatore*
          (The Troubador)

Libretto by Salvatore Cammarano (completed by Leone
Emanuele Bardare), based on the play *El Trovador* by Antonio
García Gutiérrez; first produced at the Teatro Apollo, Rome,
in 1853.

A story of love and revenge, set in northern Spain in the
fifteenth century. Manrico has been brought up by the gypsy
woman, Azucena, to believe that he is her son. In reality, he is
the brother of the Count di Luna, his rival in war and also for
the hand of Leonora, who loves Manrico. Thinking that
Manrico is the son of the gypsy who, years before, had killed
his brother, the Count orders Manrico's execution. Leonora
attempts to save him, by offering herself to the Duke and
taking poison, but the plot misfires.

This is the opera I would recommend as a test for anyone
wishing to know whether opera is for him (or her), for the
music is ravishingly beautiful, while the plot takes a bit of
swallowing.

Recommended recordings: HMV ALP 1832–3, with Jussi
Björling (Manrico), Zinka Milanov (Leonora), Leonard Warren
(Count di Luna), Fedora Barbieri (Azucena), conducted by
Renato Cellini; HMV SLS 869, with Giuseppe di Stefano
(Manrico), Maria Callas (Leonora), Rolando Panerai (Count di
Luna), Fedora Barbieri (Azucena), conducted by Herbert von
Karajan.

46   Verdi: *La Traviata*
          (The Wayward Woman)

Libretto by Francesco Maria Piave, based on the play *La
Dame aux Camélias* by Alexandre Dumas *fils*; first produced
at the Teatro La Fenice, Venice, in 1853.

The courtesan Violetta, incurably ill with consumption, falls in
love with Alfredo, and goes to live with him in the country, but
leaves him at the behest of his father, Giorgio Germont, and

returns to her former protection. She is publicly insulted by Alfredo, who returns to her months later, when he learns the truth, only to find her dying.

La Traviata is Verdi's most exquisite and romantic opera, and the music throughout is unfailingly beautiful and tuneful.

Recommended recordings: Decca SET 249–51, with Joan Sutherland (Violetta), Carlo Bergonzi (Alfredo), Robert Merrill (Germont), conducted by John Pritchard; Deutsche Grammophon 2707 103, with Ileana Cotrubas (Violetta), Placido Domingo (Alfredo), Sherrill Milnes (Germont), conducted by Carlos Kleiber; HMV SLS 960, with Beverly Sills (Violetta), Nicolai Gedda (Alfredo), Rolando Panerai (Germont), conducted by Aldo Ceccato.

47 Verdi: *Simon Boccanegra*

Libretto by Francesco Maria Piave, revised by Arrigo Boito, based on the play *Simón Boccanegra* by Antonio García Gutiérrez; first produced at the Teatro La Fenice, Venice, in 1857; revised version first performed at La Scala, Milan, in 1881.

The seafaring buccaneer Boccanegra is elected plebeian Doge of Genoa in the middle of the fourteenth century. He has had a child by the daughter of the patrician Fiesco who, when his daughter dies, swears revenge on Boccanegra. Twenty-five years later, after much plotting and intrigue, and an abortive revolt, Boccanegra is reunited with his missing child, Maria, and blesses her marriage to a political opponent, Gabriele Adorno, before dying of poison.

Recommended recordings: HMV SLS 5090, with Tito Gobbi (Boccanegra), Victoria de los Angeles (Maria), Giuseppe Campora (Gabriele), Boris Christoff (Fiesco), conducted by Gabriele Santini; Deutsche Grammophon 2709 017, with Piero Cappuccilli (Boccanegra), Mirella Freni (Maria), José Carreras (Gabriele), Nicolai Ghiaurov (Fiesco), conducted by Claudio Abbado.

48   Verdi: *Un Ballo in maschera*
(A masked ball)

Libretto by Antonio Somma, based on Eugène Scribe's libretto for Auber's opera, *Gustave III*; first produced at the Teatro Apollo, Rome, in 1859.

Riccardo, Governor of Boston at the end of the seventeenth century, is in love with Amelia, the wife of his friend and chief adviser, Renato. Thinking his wife unfaithful to him, Renato joins with conspirators to murder Riccardo. As he dies, Riccardo swears that Amelia is innocent, and forgives Renato.

The fictional characters and Boston locale were given to the opera shortly before its production, when the censorship would not allow the assassination of an historical reigning monarch to be enacted on the stage. Modern productions, however, frequently revert to Verdi's original intentions, and set the opera in eighteenth-century Sweden. Riccardo then becomes Gustave III, and Renato is Ankarstroem.

Recommended recordings: RCA SER 5710–12, with Leontyne Price (Amelia), Carlo Bergonzi (Riccardo), Robert Merrill (Renato), conducted by Erich Leinsdorf; Columbia CMS 823, with Maria Callas (Amelia), Giuseppe di Stefano (Riccardo), Tito Gobbi (Renato), conducted by Antonino Votto.

49   Verdi: *La Forza del destino*
(The force of destiny)

Libretto by Francesco Maria Piave, based on the play *Don Alvaro o La fuerza del sino* by Angel Saavedra, Duke of Rivas, and on a scene from the play *Wallensteins Lager* by Friedrich Schiller; first produced at the Imperial Theatre, St Petersburg, in 1862; revised version first produced at La Scala, Milan, in 1869.

Don Alvaro accidentally kills the father of Leonora, the woman he loves, and is pursued by her brother, Don Carlo.

Leonora seeks the advice of Padre Guardiano, a Franciscan
monk, and becomes a hermit, while Alvaro, unknown to her,
also seeks refuge in the monastery. Alvaro is forced to fight
with Carlo, whom he kills, but not before Carlo has killed his
sister, Leonora.

Recommended recordings: Decca GOS 660–2, with Zinka
Milanov (Leonora); Giuseppe di Stefano (Don Alvaro),
Leonard Warren (Don Carlo), Giorgio Tozzi (Padre
Guardiano), conducted by Fernando Previtali; RCA SER
5527–30, with Leontyne Price (Leonora), Richard Tucker (Don
Alvaro), Robert Merrill (Don Carlo), Giorgio Tozzi (Padre
Guardiano), conducted by Thomas Schippers.

50   Verdi: *Don Carlos*

Libretto by Joseph Méry and Camille du Locle, based on the
play *Don Carlos* by Schiller; first produced at the Opéra, Paris,
in 1867; revised four-act version (which omits the original Act
I) first produced at La Scala, Milan, in 1884.

Set in the sixteenth-century Spain of Philip II, the opera deals
with the marriage of Philip to Elisabeth de Valois, who was
originally betrothed to Philip's son, Don Carlos; with the
opposition of Carlos and his friend Rodrigo, Marquis of Posa,
to the King's policy in Flanders; and with the struggle for
power between church and state. The Princess Eboli, in love
with Carlos, intrigues against him, and the opera ends with
Rodrigo sacrificing his life for his friend, and with Carlos
being handed over to the Inquisition by his father, the King.

One of Verdi's most complex operas, *Don Carlos* remains
accessible and easy to listen to. It is best heard in the language
of its audience, for the highly literate libretto deserves to be
heard line for line.

Recommended recordings (there are as yet no recordings of
the opera in its original French, though one is imminent, but
only in the Italian translation authorised by Verdi): five-act
version, HMV SLS 956, with Ruggero Raimondi (Philip II),
Placido Domingo (Carlos), Sherrill Milnes (Rodrigo),

Montserrat Caballé (Elisabeth), Shirley Verrett (Eboli), conducted by Carlo Maria Giulini; four-act version, HMV Seraphim 1C 6004, with Boris Christoff (Philip II), Mario Filippeschi (Carlos), Tito Gobbi (Rodrigo), Antonietta Stella (Elisabeth), Elena Nicolai (Eboli), conducted by Gabriele Santini.

51   Verdi: *Aida*

Libretto by Camille du Locle, translated into Italian by Antonio Ghislanzoni, and based on a synopsis by Auguste Mariette; first produced at the Cairo Opera House, in 1871.

Set in Egypt in the time of the Pharaohs, the opera tells of the love of the Egyptian captain, Radames, for the Ethiopian slave Aida, daughter of Amonasro, King of Ethiopia, who is captured by the Egyptians. When Radames is condemned to death for having unwittingly betrayed military information to Amonasro, Aida chooses to die with him, while the Pharaoh's daughter, Amneris, who also loves him, fails to persuade Radames to save himself.

The greatest of grand operas, *Aida* is one of the most enjoyable as well. The march from the triumphal scene is well known outside the opera, as is the tenor aria, 'Celeste Aida'.

Recommended recordings: HMV SLS 5108, with Maria Callas (Aida), Richard Tucker (Radames), Fedora Barbieri (Amneris), Tito Gobbi (Amonasro), conducted by Tullio Serafin; Decca SET 427–9, with Leontyne Price (Aida), Jon Vickers (Radames), Rita Gorr (Amneris), Robert Merrill (Amonasro), conducted by Georg Solti.

52   Verdi: *Otello*

Libretto by Arrigo Boito, based on the play *Othello* by Shakespeare; first produced at La Scala, Milan, in 1887.

The opera follows the Shakespeare play closely, though it omits the play's first act, and sets the entire action in Cyprus.

Othello is one of the greatest of all operas, a towering dramatic masterpiece, and the role of the Moor is one which tenors approach with awe.

Recommended recordings: RCA AT303, with Ramon Vinay (Otello), Herva Nelli (Desdemona), Giuseppe Valdengo (Iago), conducted by Arturo Toscanini; RCA SER 5646–8 with Jon Vickers (Otello), Leonie Rysanek (Desdemona), Tito Gobbi (Iago), conducted by Tullio Serafin.

53   Verdi: *Falstaff*

Libretto by Arrigo Boito, based on the play *The Merry Wives of Windsor* by Shakespeare; first produced at La Scala, Milan, in 1893.

The opera follows Shakespeare's play closely, though it simplifies the plot and uses fewer characters. Sir John Falstaff is foiled in his attempt to seduce simultaneously the wives of Ford and Page, who have their revenge by holding him up to ridicule.

Recommended recordings: HMV SLS 5037, with Tito Gobbi (Falstaff), Elisabeth Schwarzkopf (Mistress Ford), Rolando Panerai (Ford), Fedora Barbieri (Mistress Quickly), conducted by Herbert von Karajan; Decca 2BB 104–6, with Geraint Evans (Falstaff), Ilva Ligabue (Mistress Ford), Robert Merrill (Ford), Giulietta Simionato (Mistress Quickly), conducted by Georg Solti.

54   Gounod: *Faust*

Libretto by Barbier and Carré, based on Goethe's *Faust*, Part One; first produced at the Théâtre-Lyrique, Paris, in 1859.

Having sold his soul to Mephistopheles in return for eternal youth, Faust seduces Marguerite and kills her brother Valentine. Marguerite gives birth to a child, and is imprisoned when she kills it. Refusing to escape from prison when urged to do so by Faust, she dies. Her soul ascends to heaven, as Faust is dragged down to hell by Mephistopheles.

The opera is very tuneful and you may be suprised at how many of the tunes you already know, e.g. the Soldiers Chorus.

Recommended recording: HMV SLS 816, with Nicolai Gedda (Faust), Victoria de los Angeles (Marguerite), Boris Christoff (Mephistopheles), Ernst Blanc (Valentine), conducted by André Cluytens.

Other operas by Gounod include *Mireille* and *Roméo et Juliette*.

55   Offenbach: *La Belle Hélène*
(Beautiful Helen)

Libretto by Meilhac and Halévy; first produced at the Théâtre des Variétés, Paris, in 1864.

An operetta which satirically re-tells the legend of Helen of Troy, in which Paris and Helen, aided by Calchas, the Spartan High Priest, outwit Helen's husband, Menelaus, King of Sparta, and sail off to Troy. The music is high-spirited, witty and immensely tuneful.

Recommended recording: Everest S 458, with Janine Linda (Helen), André Dran (Paris), Roger Giraud (Menelaus), conducted by Réné Leibowitz.

56   Offenbach: *Les Contes d'Hoffmann*
(Tales of Hoffmann)

Libretto by Barbier and Carré, based on three stories by E.T.A. Hoffmann: *Der Sandmann, Geschichte vom verlorenen*

Spiegelbilde, and *Rat Krespel*; first produced at the
Opéra-Comique, Paris, in 1881.

The poet Hoffmann regales his companions with three stories
of his great loves, involving Olympia, the doll whom his evil
genius persuades him is real; Antonia, the consumptive
daughter of Councillor Crespel; and the Venetian courtesan,
Giulietta. All three are aspects of his one and only love, the
opera singer, Stella, whom he loses to his rival Lindorf,
another manifestation of Hoffmann's evil genius.

The Tales of Hoffmann, though difficult to stage, is a
fascinating work. The Barcarolle is well known, but the entire
score is equally easy to listen to.

Recommended recordings: HMV SLS with Nicolai Gedda
(Hoffmann), Gianna d'Angelo (Olympia), Victoria de los
Angeles (Antonia), Elisabeth Schwarzkopf (Giulietta),
conducted by André Cluytens; Decca SET 545–7, with Placido
Domingo (Hoffmann), and all three soprano roles sung by
Joan Sutherland, conducted by Richard Bonynge.

Les Contes d'Hoffmann is Offenbach's only opera. His
operettas include *La Vie Parisienne* and *Orpheus in the
Underworld*.

57 Smetana: *Prodaná Nevěsta*
(The Bartered Bride)

Libretto by Karel Sabina; first produced at the Provisional
Theatre, Prague, in 1866.

A love story set in a Bohemian village in the middle of the
nineteenth century. Mařenka is in love with Jenik, but her
parents want her to marry a simpleton named Vašek, the son
of Tobias Micha. Jenik accepts money to renounce Mařenka
so long as she marries the son of Tobias Micha, and it
transpires that he, Jenik, is Micha's son by a previous
marriage. All ends happily.

This is the favourite opera of the Czechs, and a very engaging
romantic comedy.

Recommended recording: Supraphon SUAST 50397–9, with Drahomira Tikalová (Mařenka), Ivo Zidek (Jenik), Oldrich Kovár (Vašek), conducted by Zdenek Chalabala.

Smetana's other operas include *Dalibor*, *The Kiss* and *The Devil's Wall*.

58   Johann Strauss: *Die Fledermaus*
                    (The Bat)

Libretto by Karl Haffner and Richard Genée, based on the comedy *Le Réveillon* by Meilhac and Halévy; first produced at the Theater an der Wien, Vienna, in 1874.

Eisenstein, instead of going to prison for five days for a minor offence, is persuaded by his friend Dr Falke to accompany him to a party being given by Prince Orlovsky. Eisenstein's wife Rosalinde, whose admirer Alfred, an opera singer, has been arrested as Eisenstein when found tête-à-tête with Rosalinde, arrives in disguise at the party, at Falke's instigation, to find her husband flirting with their maid, Adele, who has gone under an assumed name and wearing one of Rosalinde's gowns. Eisenstein is tricked into attempting a seduction of his disguised wife. Everything has been part of Falke's tortuous plan of revenge on Eisenstein, for a joke which Eisenstein had played on Falke, holding him up to ridicule. All misunderstandings are cleared up the next morning at the prison.

Hard-hearted is the person who can resist Strauss's lilting waltz rhythms and his gaiety tinged with melancholy.

Recommended recordings: Decca DAP 585–6, with Hilde Gueden (Rosalinde), Julius Patzak (Eisenstein), Anton Dermota (Alfred), Alfred Poell (Dr Falke), Wilma Lipp (Adele), conducted by Clemens Krauss; HMV RLS 728, with Elisabeth Schwarzkopf (Rosalinde), Nicolai Gedda (Eisenstein), Helmut Krebs (Alfred), Erich Kunz (Dr Falke), Rita Streich (Adele), conducted by Herbert von Karajan.

59   Johann Strauss: *Der Zigeunerbaron*
        (The Gypsy Baron)

Libretto by Ignaz Schnitzer, altered from a libretto by Maurus
Jókai, based on his story, *Saffi*; first produced at the Theater
an der Wien, Vienna, in 1885.

The action takes place in Hungary and in Vienna in the
middle of the eighteenth century, and tells how Sándor
Barinkay returns to claim his property only to find it annexed
by Zsupán, a wealthy pig-breeder. He falls in love with a
gypsy girl, Saffi, who in due course turns out to be a princess.
As a commoner, although given the title of Gypsy Baron,
Sandor feels he must renounce Saffi. He enlists in the army,
and so distinguishes himself in battle that he is raised to the
ranks of the nobility. He and Saffi can now marry.

The Gypsy Baron contains some of Strauss's best-known and
most entertaining melodies.

Recommended recording: HMV SXDW 3046, with Nicolai
Gedda (Sándor Barinkay), Elisabeth Schwarzkopf (Saffi),
Erich Kunz (Zsupán), conducted by Otto Ackermann.

60   Ponchielli: *La Gioconda*
        (The Joyous Girl)

Libretto by Arrigo Boito (under the pseudonym 'Tobia Gorrio',
which is an anagram of his name), based on the play *Angelo,
Tyran de Padoue* by Victor Hugo; first produced at La Scala,
Milan, in 1876.

La Gioconda, a street singer in Venice, is in love with Enzo
Grimaldo who in turn loves Laura, wife of the nobleman
Alvise. When La Gioconda rejects the advances of Barnaba, a
spy of the Inquisition, he has her mother arrested. Laura
successfully pleads for the old woman's release, in return for
which La Gioconda helps Laura and Enzo to escape together
from Venice, and kills herself rather than submit to Barnaba.

This exotic and melodramatic opera contains the 'Dance of the Hours' popularised in Walt Disney's *Fantasia*.

Recommended recording: Decca SET 364–5, with Renata Tebaldi (La Gioconda), Carlo Bergonzi (Enzo Grimaldo), Marilyn Horne (Laura), Robert Merrill (Barnaba), conducted by Lamberto Gardelli.

61   Bizet: *Carmen*

Libretto by Meilhac and Halévy, after the novel *Carmen* by Prosper Merimée; first produced at the Opéra-Comique, Paris, in 1875.

In early nineteenth-century Seville, the gypsy girl Carmen finds it easy to seduce a corporal, Don José, away from his fiancée, Micaela. Don José abandons his regiment to be with Carmen, and takes to the mountains with her and a group of smugglers. However, when Carmen tires of him and leaves him for the toreador Escamillo, Don José kills her.

Carmen is, deservedly, one of the most popular of all operas. Its music reached an even wider audience when used in the stage and film adaptation, *Carmen Jones*.

Recommended recording: HMV SLS 913, with Maria Callas (Carmen), Nicolai Gedda (Don José), Robert Massard (Escamillo), Andrea Guiot (Micaela), conducted by Georges Prêtre.

62   Mussorgsky: *Boris Godunov*

Libretto by the composer, based on Pushkin's drama, *The Comedy of the Distress of the Muscovite State, of Tsar Boris, and of Grishka Otrepiev*; first produced at the Imperial Theatre, St Petersburg, in 1874.

The opera tells of how Boris Godunov becomes Tsar of Russia in 1598, and of the events leading to his death, including an uprising led by a Pretender to the throne, a young religious novice, Grigory, who claims to be the Dmitry whom Boris had murdered in order to attain the throne.

Boris Godunov is the most famous, and most spectacular of Russian operas.

Recommended recordings: revised version arranged and re-orchestrated by Rimsky-Korsakov, HMV SLS 5072, with Boris Christoff (Boris), Nicolai Gedda (Grigory), conducted by Issay Dobrowen; original version, HMV SLS 1000, with Martti Talvela (Boris), Nicolai Gedda (Grigory), conducted by Jerzy Semkov.

Mussorgsky's other operas are *Khovanshchina* and *Sorochinsk Fair.*

63 Tchaikovsky: *Eugene Onegin*

Libretto by the composer and Konstantin Shilovsky, based on the dramatic poem of the same name by Pushkin; first produced at the Little Theatre of the Imperial College of Music, Moscow, in 1879.

The action takes place in and around St Petersburg in the early nineteenth century. Tatiana, a young and impressionable girl, confesses her love for Onegin, who coldly and formally rejects her. Onegin flirts with Olga, Tatiana's sister and the fiancée of Onegin's friend Lensky. Lensky challenges Onegin to a duel and is killed. Six years later, at a ball in St Petersburg, Onegin falls in love with a beautiful woman whom he is astonished to find is Tatiana, now married to Prince Gremin. He confesses his love, but it is now her turn to reject him, although in fact she loves him still.

Anyone who responds to Tchaikovsky's romantic symphonies will enjoy this tuneful lyrical opera. Its two dance movements are popular concert pieces.

Recommended recording: HMV SLS 951, with Yuri Masurok (Onegin), Galina Vishnevskaya (Tatiana), Vladimir Atlantov (Lensky), conducted by Mstislav Rostropovich.

Tchaikovsky's other operas include *The Queen of Spades* and *The Maid of Orleans.*

64 Massenet: *Manon*

Libretto by Henri Meilhac and Philippe Gille, based on the novel, *L'Histoire du Chevalier Des Grieux et de Manon Lescaut* by Abbé Prévost; first produced at the Opéra-Comique, Paris, in 1884.

The Chevalier des Grieux elopes with young Manon Lescaut whom he has met when she was on her way to a convent. Seduced away from Des Grieux by a richer admirer, Manon returns to him when he is about to enter the priesthood. At a gambling house, Des Grieux is accused of cheating, and Manon is arrested, charged with being an immoral woman, and sentenced to deportation. Manon dies in the arms of Des Grieux, who has attempted to rescue her.

This is nineteenth-century French opera at its most romantic; an easy opera to get to know.

Recommended recording: HMV SLS 800, with Beverly Sills (Manon), Nicolai Gedda (Des Grieux), conducted by Julius Rudel.

65 Massenet: *Werther*

Libretto by Blau, Millet and Hartmann, based on the novel *Die Leiden des jungen Werthers* by Goethe; first produced at the Hofoper, Vienna, in 1892.

Werther is in love with Charlotte who marries Albert, to whom she had been betrothed before meeting Werther. Werther, in despair at losing Charlotte, kills himself.

Gloomier than the same composer's *Manon*, *Werther* will still repay examination.

Recommended recording: HMV SLS 5105, with Nicolai Gedda (Werther), Victoria de los Angeles (Charlotte), Roger Soyer (Albert), conducted by Georges Prêtre.

Massenet's other operas include *Le Roi de Lahore* and *Thaïs*.

66   Humperdinck: *Hänsel und Gretel*

Libretto by Adelheid Wette, based on the story in the Grimm
brothers' *Kinder- und Hausmärchen*; first performed at
Weimar, in 1893.

The opera tells the familiar story of Hansel and Gretel who are
captured by a witch who turns little children into gingerbread.
They outwit her, and rescue the bewitched children, in the
process turning the witch herself into gingerbread. This is an
opera which has proved popular with children.

Recommended recording: RCA ARL2 0637, with Anna Moffo
(Hansel), Helen Donath (Gretel), Christa Ludwig (Witch),
conducted by Kurt Eichhorn.

67   Leoncavallo: *Pagliacci*
(Clowns)

Libretto by the composer; first produced at the Teatro dal
Verme, Milan, in 1892.

Canio, the leader of a troupe of travelling players, is informed
by Tonio, another member of the troupe, that his wife, Nedda,
is unfaithful to him. During a performance, Canio loses control
of himself, demands that his wife, playing opposite him,
reveal the name of her lover and, when she refuses, stabs her.
Her lover, Silvio, leaps on to the stage to come to her aid, and
he too is killed by Canio.

Pagliacci, usually performed together with Mascagni's
Cavalleria Rusticana, contains the popular tenor aria, 'Vesti la
giubba' (On with the motley).

Recommended recordings: HMV SLS 819, with Giuseppe di
Stefano (Canio), Maria Callas (Nedda), Tito Gobbi (Tonio),
Rolando Panerai (Silvio), conducted by Tullio Serafin;
Deutsche Grammophon 2709 020f, with Carlo Bergonzi
(Canio), Joan Carlyle (Nedda), Giuseppe Taddei (Tonio),
Rolando Panerai (Silvio), conducted by Herbert von Karajan.

68   Puccini: *Manon Lescaut*

Libretto by Giacosa, Illica and others, based on the novel, *L'Histoire du Chevalier Des Grieux et de Manon Lescaut* by Abbé Prévost; first produced at the Teatro Regio, Turin, in 1893.

The plot is basically the same as that of Massenet's *Manon*, except that Manon is deported to Louisiana, and Des Grieux goes with her. Fleeing from New Orleans, they attempt to cross a desert on foot, and Manon dies in the arms of Des Grieux.

The earliest opera by Puccini to achieve lasting success, *Manon Lescaut* is highly dramatic, and the composer's style is, as it was to remain, simple and accessible.

Recommended recording: HMV SLS 962, with Montserrat Caballé (Manon), Placido Domingo (Des Grieux), conducted by Bruno Bartoletti.

69   Puccini: *La Bohème*
(The Bohemians)

Libretto by Giacosa and Illica, based on the novel, *Scènes de la vie de Bohème* by Henri Murger; first produced at the Teatro Regio, Turin, in 1896.

Rodolfo, one of a group of Bohemian artists sharing a Paris attic, falls in love with their neighbour, Mimi, a seamstress. While the painter Marcello has a light-hearted affair with Musetta, Mimi and Rodolfo find their relationship difficult to sustain, and they part. Mimi returns only when she is dying of consumption.

This popular and sentimental piece is the favourite opera of many, and a suitable work to break one's operatic teeth on! The tenor aria, known in English as 'Your tiny hand is frozen' is justly famous.

Recommended recordings: HV SLS 896, with Victoria de los Angeles (Mimi), Jussi Björling (Rodolfo), Lucine Amara (Musetta), Robert Merrill (Marcello), conducted by Sir Thomas Beecham; Decca SET 565–6, with Mirella Freni (Mimi), Luciano Pavarotti (Rodolfo), Elizabeth Harwood (Musetta), Rolando Panerai (Marcello), conducted by Herbert von Karajan.

70   Puccini: *Tosca*

Libretto by Giacosa and Illica, based on the play *La Tosca* by Sardou; first produced at the Teatro Costanzi, Rome, in 1900.

The action takes place in Rome in 1800. The painter Cavaradossi and the opera singer Tosca are lovers. Cavaradossi, a supporter of the Republican cause, helps a political prisoner to escape, and is himself arrested and tortured by Scarpia, the chief of police who lusts after Tosca. Scarpia tells Tosca she can save Cavaradossi's life only by giving herself to him, in return for which he will arrange a mock execution of Cavaradossi. Tosca agrees, but stabs and kills Scarpia as soon as he has signed a travel permit for herself and Cavaradossi to leave Rome. She hurries to inform Cavaradossi of the mock execution, but when the shots ring out Cavaradossi falls to the ground: Scarpia had tricked her. Distraught, Tosca flings herself to her death from the battlements of the prison.

Puccini's highly popular melodrama contains the famous soprano aria, 'Vissi d'arte', and the at least equally well-known tenor aria 'E lucevan le stella'.

Recommended recordings: HMV SLS 826, with Maria Callas (Tosca), Tito Gobbi (Scarpia), Giuseppe di Stefano (Cavaradossi), conducted by Victor De Sabata; Decca 5BB 123–4, with Leontyne Price (Tosca), Giuseppe Taddei (Scarpia), Giuseppe di Stefano (Cavaradossi), conducted by Herbert von Karajan.

71   Puccini: *Madama Butterfly*

Libretto by Giacosa and Illica, based on the play *Madame Butterfly* by David Belasco, which in turn was based on a story by John Luther Long; first produced at La Scala, Milan, in 1904.

The action takes place in Nagasaki at the beginning of this century. The American naval officer, Lieutenant Pinkerton, goes through a ceremony of marriage with a young Japanese geisha girl, known as Butterfly, despite the expressed misgivings of Sharpless, the American Consul. When Pinkerton returns to America, Butterfly is convinced that he will return to her. When he returns, three years later, he is accompanied by an American wife. Overcome with grief, Butterfly kills herself.

The third of the three most popular Puccini operas, *Madama Butterfly* contains what is probably the most famous of soprano arias, 'Un bel dì' (One Fine Day).

Recommended recordings: Decca SET 584–6 with Mirella Freni (Butterfly), Luciano Pavarotti (Pinkerton), Robert Kerns (Sharpless), conducted by Herbert von Karajan; HMV SLS 927, with Renata Scotto (Butterfly), Carlo Bergonzi (Pinkerton), Rolando Panerai (Sharpless), conducted by Sir John Barbirolli.

72   Puccini: *La Fanciulla del West*
(The Girl of the Golden West)

Libretto by Civinini and Zangarini, based on the play *The Girl of the Golden West* by David Belasco; first produced at the Metropolitan Opera, New York, in 1910.

The opera is set in the Californian mining camps of the mid-nineteenth century. Minnie, owner of the local saloon, is loved by the Sheriff, Jack Rance, but is herself in love with a mysterious stranger, Dick Johnson, who turns out to be the notorious bandit, Ramerrez. Minnie helps Ramerrez to escape from the Sheriff, but he is finally captured and about to be hanged when she successfully pleads for his life, and they leave to start a new life together. The opera contains in Act III, a popular tenor aria, 'Ch'ella mi creda libero e lontano', sung by Ramerrez as he thinks he is about to be hanged.

Recommended recording: Deutsche Grammophon 2709 078, with Carol Neblett (Minnie), Placido Domingo (Dick Johnson), Sherrill Milnes (Jack Rance), conducted by Zubin Mehta.

73   Puccini: *Turandot*

Libretto by Adami and Simoni, based on the play *Turandot* by Gozzi; first produced at La Scala, Milan, in 1926.

Puccini died before he had completed the final act of the opera, which was completed by Franco Alfano. In the old Peking of legend, the Princess Turandot poses riddles for her suitors to answer. When they fail, they are beheaded. The disguised Prince Calaf suceeds in answering the riddles, but gives Turandot a chance to reject him. If she can discover his name by morning, he is content to die. Turandot tortures Calaf's faithful slave-girl, Liù, in an attempt to discover his name, but Liù kills herself rather than reveal it. Turandot's eyes are opened to the power of true love, and she accepts Calaf. One of Puccini's most popular tenor arias, 'Nessun dorma' (None shall sleep) is sung by Calaf at the beginning of Act III.

Recommended recordings: Decca SET 561–3, with Joan Sutherland (Turandot), Luciano Pavarotti (Calaf), Montserrat Caballé (Liù), conducted by Zubin Mehta; RCA SER 5643–5, with Birgit Nilsson (Turandot), Jussi Björling (Calaf), Renata Tebaldi (Liù), conducted by Francesco Molinari-Pradelli.

74   Debussy: *Pelléas et Mélisande*

Libretto, a shortened version of the play *Pelléas et Mélisande,* by Maeterlinck; first produced at the Opéra-Comique, Paris, in 1902.

Golaud brings home to the court of his father King Arkel of Allemonde a mysterious girl, Mélisande, whom he marries. Mélisande and Pelléas, Golaud's half-brother, fall in love. Pelléas is killed by Golaud. Mélisande dies after giving birth to a child.

Pelléas et Mélisande is important in the history of opera, but is something of an acquired taste. I would not recommend it to newcomers to the world of opera.

Recommended recording: Decca SET 277–9, with Camille Maurane (Pelléas), Erna Spoorenberg (Mélisande), George London (Golaud), conducted by Ernest Ansermet.

75   Mascagni: *Cavalleria Rusticana*
(Rustic Chivalry)

Libretto by Giuseppe Targioni-Tozzetti and Guido Menasci, based on Verga's play, *Cavalleria Rusticana,* which is a dramatisation of the author's story of the same title; first produced at the Teatro Costanzi, Rome, in 1890.

The action takes place in a Sicilian village where Santuzza, made pregnant by Turiddu, is jealous and distraught when he deserts her for Lola, the wife of Alfio. Santuzza reveals his wife's infidelity to Alfio who challenges Turiddu to a duel and kills him.

This operatic melodrama can be enjoyed by all, and contains the famous Easter Hymn and orchestral Intermezzo.

Recommended Recordings: HMV SLS 819, with Maria Callas (Santuzza), Giuseppe di Stefano (Turiddu), Rolando Panerai

(Alfio), conducted by Tullio Serafin; Deutsche Grammophon 2709 020, with Fiorenza Cossotto (Santuzza), Carlo Bergonzi (Turiddu), Giangiacomo Guelfi (Alfio), conducted by Herbert von Karajan.

Mascagni's other operas include *L'Amico Fritz*.

76   Richard Strauss: *Elektra*

Libretto by Hugo von Hofmannsthal, after his play which is based on the *Elektra* of Sophocles; first produced at the Hofoper, Dresden, in 1909.

Elektra mourns the death of her father Agamemnon, murdered by her mother Klytemnestra, and tries to persuade her sister Chrysothemis to help her avenge it. Their brother Orest, thought to be dead, returns and kills both Klytemnestra and her lover Aegisth. Elektra exults in a wild dance of triumph, and then collapses.

A powerful and dramatic work, *Elektra* has something of the mood of Greek tragedy.

Recommended recording: Decca SET 354–5, with Birgit Nilsson (Elektra), Regina Resnik (Klytemnestra), Marie Collier (Chrysothemis), Tom Krause (Orest), conducted by Georg Solti.

77   Richard Strauss: *Salomé*

Libretto an abridgment of the German translation by Hedwig Lachmann of the play *Salomé* by Oscar Wilde; first produced at the Hofoper, Dresden, in 1905.

Jochanaan (John the Baptist), imprisoned by Herod for proclaiming the coming of the Messiah, attracts the lustful attention of Herod's daughter Salomé. Salomé agrees to dance for her father on condition that he will give her whatever she asks for. Herod agrees, and after she has danced Salomé asks for the head of Jochanaan. Herod is forced to produce it for her, and the depraved Salomé fondles and kisses it until Herod, in disgust, orders his soldiers to kill her, which they do by crushing her to death beneath their shields. Salomé's final solo, with the head of Jochanaan, is the highlight of the opera.

Recommended recording: Decca SET 228–9, with Birgit Nilsson (Salomé), Gerhard Stolze (Herod), Eberhard Wächter (Jochanaan), conducted by Georg Solti.

78   Richard Strauss: *Der Rosenkavalier*
(The Cavalier of the Rose)

Libretto by Hugo von Hofmannsthal; first produced at the Hofoper, Dresden, in 1911.

A comedy, set in eighteenth-century Vienna, about the amorous intrigues of the Princess of Werdenberg, known as the Marschallin (since her husband is a Field-Marshal in the army), her cousin, Baron Ochs, the young Count Octavian and Sophie, the daughter of Faninal, a merchant. Octavian, the lover of the Marschallin, falls in love with Sophie, and hatches a plot to discredit Baron Ochs who is engaged to marry the girl. His plan succeeds only when it is helped along by the Marschallin who wisely releases Octavian, and gives the young couple her blessing.

The music is sumptuous, lilting waltzes and soaring lyrical lines for the sopranos predominating.

Recommended recordings: HMV SLS 810, with Elisabeth Schwarzkopf (Marschallin), Christa Ludwig (Octavian), Otto Edelmann (Ochs), Teresa Stich-Randall (Sophie), conducted by Herbert von Karajan; there is an abridged recording on World Records SH 181–2, with a famous cast of the 1920s and 30s, recorded in 1934; Lotte Lehmann (Marschallin), Maria Olszewska (Octavian), Richard Mayr (Ochs), Elisabeth Schumann (Sophie), conducted by Robert Heger.

79   Richard Strauss: *Die Frau ohne Schatten*

(The Woman Without a Shadow)

Libretto by Hugo von Hofmannsthal, based on his story of the same title; first produced at the Hofoper, Vienna, in 1919.

A story, set in legendary times, of an Empress who, only half human, cannot bear a child. Unless she can find a shadow, and thus the ability to bear children, her husband the Emperor will be turned to stone. She comes to earth, to the house of Barak the Dyer, whose wife is persuaded to exchange her shadow for riches. Finally, the Empress learns human compassion and refuses to deprive the Dyer's wife of her shadow, for which she is rewarded by the gift of a shadow from the world of spirits.

This is not an easy opera, but it repays study, and Strauss's orchestration is masterly.

Recommended recording: Decca GOS 554–7, with Hans Hopf (Emperor), Leonie Rysanek (Empress), Paul Schoeffler (Barak), Christel Goltz (Barak's Wife), conducted by Karl Böhm.

80   Richard Strauss: *Arabella*

Libretto by Hugo von Hofmannsthal; first produced at the Hofoper, Dresden, in 1933.

In nineteenth-century Vienna, the impoverished Count Waldner plans to marry his daughter to a wealthy landowner, Mandryka, whom she loves, but the happy outcome is delayed by a number of complications and misunderstandings, mainly caused by the fact that Arabella's younger sister, Zdenka, has been brought up as a boy, since the Waldner family could not afford to introduce two girls into Viennese society.

Recommended recording: Decca GOS 571–3, with Lisa della

Casa (Arabella), George London (Mandryka), Hilde Gueden
(Zdenka), conducted by Georg Solti.

Strauss's other operas include *Die Liebe der Danae, Die
Schweigsame Frau* and *Capriccio.*

81 Giordano: *Andrea Chénier*

Libretto by Luigi Illica; first produced at La Scala, Milan,
1896.

Set in Paris at the time of the French Revolution, the opera
tells of the love of Madeleine for the poet Andrea Chénier.
She in turn is loved by Gérard, a former servant in her
household who, motivated largely by jealousy of Chénier,
denounces him to the revolutionary tribunal. Madeleine
chooses to go to the guillotine with Chénier.

This is late nineteenth-century Italian opera at its greatest, not
subtle but certainly exciting.

Recommended recording: RCA RLO 2046, with Placido
Domingo (Chénier), Renata Scotto (Madeleine), Sherrill
Milnes (Gérard), conducted by James Levine.

82 Lehár: *Die Lustige Witwe*
(The Merry Widow)

Libretto by Viktor Léon and Leo Stein, based on the play,
L'Attaché by Henri Meilhac; first produced at the Theater an
der Wien, Vienna, in 1905.

The plot concerns the attempts of the Pontevedrian
Ambassador in Paris to effect a marriage between the rich
widow Hanna and the diplomat Prince Danilo in order to stop
Hanna's fortune from leaving Pontevedro. Hanna and Danilo
love each other, but each is reluctant to be the first to admit
the fact. Needless to say, all ends happily.

The Merry Widow is deservedly popular, and Lehár's music is exquisitely scored. You will probably know most of the tunes, even if you have never seen the operetta.

Recommended recordings: HMV SXDW 3045, with Elisabeth Schwarzkopf (Hanna), Erich Kunz (Danilo), conducted by Otto Ackermann; Deutsche Grammophon 2707 070, with Elizabeth Harwood (Hanna), René Kollo (Danilo), conducted by Herbert von Karajan.

Lehár's other operettas include *The Land of Smiles, The Count of Luxembourg, Frasquita, Paganini, Friederike* and *Giuditta*.

83   Ravel: *L'Enfant et les sortilèges*
(The Bewitched Child)

Libretto by Colette; first produced at the Opera House, Monte Carlo, in 1925.

The child's books, toys and his nursery furniture rebel against his cruel treatment of them, and combine to torment him. They relent when he shows compassion for a baby squirrel. This is an enchanting little opera, and suitable for children.

Recommended recording: Decca SDD 168, with Flora Wend (Enfant), and the roles of the various creatures shared by, among others, Suzanne Danco, Geneviève Touraine and Hughes Cuénod, conducted by Ernest Ansermet.

84   Ravel: *L'Heure Espagnole*
(The Spanish Hour)

Libretto by Franc-Nohain, based on his own comedy; first produced at the Opéra-Comique, Paris, in 1911.

A comedy about the escapades of Concepción, wife of the clockmaker Torquemada, who entertains her lovers during her husband's daily absence to wind the town clocks.

Ravel's score is short on tunes, but exquisite in its instrumentation.

Recommended recording: Decca ECS 786, with Suzanne Danco (Concepción), conducted by Ernest Ansermet.

85 Stravinsky: *Oedipus Rex*
(King Oedipus)

Libretto by Jean Cocteau, based on the *Oedipus Tyrannus* of Sophocles; first performed, as an oratorio, in Paris in 1927; first produced on the stage at the Staatsoper, Vienna, in 1928.

A Narrator describes the various events, which are then enacted. Oedipus confesses to the crimes of killing his father and, unwittingly, marrying his mother, Jocasta. He has blinded himself in self-punishment, and is banished for his crimes.

Stravinsky's music impressively underlines the text; this is modern music which is easy to comprehend.

Recommended recording: Decca SET 616, with Peter Pears (Oedipus), Kerstin Meyer (Jocasta), Alec McCowen (Narrator), conducted by Georg Solti.

86 Stravinsky: *The Rake's Progress*

Libretto by W. H. Auden and Chester Kallman; first produced at the Teatro La Fenice, Venice, in 1951.

Tom Rakewell leaves his beloved Anne to go to London, when offered the prospect of great wealth by the Devil, in the guise of Nick Shadow. The opera recounts Tom's progress through profligacy to madness.

Stravinsky has written music of easy charm, though little of it remains to haunt the ear of memory.

Recommended recording: CBS 77304, with Alexander Young (Tom), Judith Raskin (Anne), John Reardon (Nick Shadow), conducted by the composer.

87   Berg: *Wozzeck*

Libretto by the composer, based on the play *Woyzeck* by Georg Büchner; first produced at the Staatsoper, Berlin, in 1925.

The simple-minded soldier, Wozzeck, is confused by his surroundings, his fellow-men and their inhumanity to one another. His mistress, Marie, is unfaithful to him, and in a fit of madness he stabs her, and then drowns in an attempt to recover the knife he has thrown into the lake.

Do not attempt to separate music from drama as you listen to this absorbing work, for music and drama are one.

Recommended recording: Deutsche Grammophon 2707 023, with Dietrich Fischer-Dieskau (Wozzeck), Evelyn Lear (Marie), conducted by Karl Böhm.

88   Berg: *Lulu*

Libretto by the composer, based on the plays *Erdgeist* and *Die Büchse der Pandora* by Wedekind; first produced, in the unfinished state in which the composer left it, at the Opera House, Zurich, in 1937. The opera has been completed from Berg's sketches, and productions now usually present the drama in its entirety.

Lulu is a *femme fatale* who, after ruining the lives of most of those around her makes her way to London, where she becomes a prostitute and a victim of Jack the Ripper.

Musically, *Lulu* is a work for the connoisseur. Do not attempt it until you have heard several other operas. Approach Berg first through *Wozzeck*.

Recommended recording: Deutsche Grammophon 2709 029, with Evelyn Lear (Lulu), conducted by Karl Böhm.

89   Gershwin: *Porgy and Bess*

Libretto by Du Bose, Heyward and Ira Gershwin, based on the play *Porgy* by Du Bose and Dorothy Heyward; first produced at the Colonial Theatre, Boston, in 1935.

An opera about the inhabitants of a negro tenement in Charleston, South Carolina. Porgy, a cripple, is in love with Bess, who is lured away to New York by the gambler, Sportin' Life. Porgy kills his rival, Crown, and sets out for New York to find Bess.

Musically, Gershwin's score is uneven, but it contains many splendid tunes, among them 'Summertime' and 'I got plenty o' nothing'.

Recommended recording: Decca SET 609–11, with Willard White (Porgy), Leona Mitchell (Bess), conducted by Lorin Maazel.

90   Weill: *Die Dreigroschenoper*
(The Threepenny Opera)

Libretto by Bertolt Brecht, a modern rewriting of *The Beggar's Opera* by Pepusch; first produced at the Theater am Schiffbauerdamm, Berlin, in 1928.

The plot follows that of its model, with the action updated to Soho, London, at the beginning of the twentieth century, and the social comment of the original made more explicit.

Recommended recording: CBS 77268, with Erich Schellow (Macheath), Johanna von Kóczián (Polly), Inge Wolffberg (Lucy), and the composer's widow, Lotte Lenya, as Jenny, conducted by Wilhelm Brückner-Rüggeberg.

91 Weill: *Aufstieg und Fall der Stadt Mahagonny*
(Rise and Fall of the City of Mahagonny)

Libretto by Bertolt Brecht; first produced in Leipzig in 1930.

A satirical parable about greed, materialism, and modern capitalist society, concerning Jimmy Mahoney, a lumberjack, his friends, and his mistress, Jenny.

Recommended recording: CBS 77341, with Heinz Saverbaum (Jimmy), Lotte Lenya (Jenny), conducted by Wilhelm Brückner-Rüggeberg.

92 Tippett: *The Midsummer Marriage*

Libretto by the composer; first produced at the Royal Opera House, Covent Garden, London, in 1955.

An allegorical story concerning the quest of two young lovers, Mark and Jennifer, for a satisfactory relationship. The action veers between the practical and the mythological, and is played out against the background of a timeless English summer.

This is Tippett's first opera, and worthy to stand beside the best of Benjamin Britten

Recommended recording: Philips 6703 027, with Alberto Remedios (Mark), Joan Carlyle (Jennifer), conducted by Colin Davis.

Tippett's other operas are *King Priam, The Knot Garden* and *The Ice-Break*.

93 Barber: *Vanessa*

Libretto by Gian Carlo Menotti; first produced at the Metropolitan Opera, New York, in 1958.

A romantic opera about Vanessa, who has waited for twenty years for the return of her lover, Anatol. When Anatol arrives, he is the son of the man she expected, and Vanessa's rival for him is her own niece. Vanessa and Anatol marry, leaving the niece, Erika, now to wait alone for a new love.

Samuel Barber writes music which falls easily on the ear, and is dramatically apposite.

Recommended recording: RCA RLO 2094, with Eleanor Steber (Vanessa), Nicolai Gedda (Anatol), Rosalind Elias (Erika), conducted by Dimitri Mitropoulos.

94   Menotti: *The Consul*

Libretto by the composer; first produced in Philadelphia, USA, in 1950.

The action takes place in an unnamed police state in Europe, and concerns the efforts of Magda Sorel to obtain exit visas for herself and her husband who is wanted by the secret police. When her husband John is arrested, Magda kills herself.

Recommended recording: Capitol OD 1950, with Patricia Neway (Magda Sorel), conducted by Lehmann Engel.

95   Britten: *Peter Grimes*

Libretto by Montagu Slater, based on the poem 'The Borough' by George Crabbe; first produced at Sadler's Wells Theatre, London, in 1945.

In a fishing village in Suffolk, Grimes is considered something of an outcast by the other villagers. He has lost a boy apprentice at sea in an accident, and when he takes on another apprentice, local feeling grows against him. Ellen Orford, the local school mistress, befriends him, but when

Grimes's new apprentice dies at sea Grimes loses his reason, and finds that death for himself too is the only way out.

Peter Grimes is Britten's masterpiece, and one of the most successful operas written in the last fifty years.

Recommended recording: Decca SXL 2150–2 with Peter Pears (Peter Grimes), Claire Watson (Ellen Orford), conducted by the composer.

96   Britten: *Billy Budd*

Libretto by E. M. Forster and Eric Crozier, based on the novella by Hermann Melville; first produced at the Royal Opera House, Covent Garden, London, in 1951.

The opera, which has an all-male cast, is set on board a British warship during Napoleonic times. The beauty and innocence of Billy, pressed into service from a merchant ship, excites the resentment and jealousy of the master-at-arms, Claggart, who falsely accuses him of treachery. Billy inadvertently kills Claggart, and Captain Vere finds himself unable to save Billy from a sentence of death.

This is a moving and impressive work.

Recommended recording: Decca SET 379–81, with Peter Glossop (Billy Budd), Peter Pears (Captain Vere), Michael Langdon (Claggart), conducted by the composer.

97   Britten: *A Midsummer Night's Dream*

Libretto by the composer and Peter Pears, based on Shakespeare's play, *A Midsummer Night's Dream*; first produced at the Jubilee Hall, Aldeburgh, Suffolk, England, in 1960.

Though many scenes have had to be omitted or truncated, the plot of the opera follows that of the play very closely. If you enjoy Shakespeare's romantic comedy, you will certainly have no trouble appreciating Britten's opera.

Recommended recording: Decca SET 338–40, with Alfred Deller (Oberon), Elisabeth Harwood (Titania), Owen Brannigan (Bottom), conducted by the composer.

98 Britten: *Death in Venice*

Libretto by Myfanwy Piper, based on the story *Der Tod in Venedig* by Thomas Mann; first produced at the Maltings, Snape, Suffolk, in 1973.

Aschenbach, a famous writer, is surprised to find himself attracted by a boy he sees on the beach at the Lido. He attempts to escape from Venice, but is kept in the city by a cholera scare. While watching Tadzio playing with other boys on the beach, Aschenbach collapses and dies.

This is Britten's last opera and an impressive work, though it lacks the popular touch of *Peter Grimes.*

Recommended recording: Decca SET 581–3, with Peter Pears (Aschenbach), and various other characters sung by John Shirley-Quirk, conducted by Steuart Bedford.

Britten's other operas include *Gloriana, Albert Herring, The Rape of Lucretia* and *Owen Wingrave.*

99 Bernstein: *West Side Story*

Libretto by Stephen Sondheim and Arthur Laurents, suggested by Shakespeare's *Romeo and Juliet*; first produced at the Winter Garden Theatre, New York, in 1957.

This American musical tells a story about gang warfare among the youths of New York's upper West Side, loosely based on the Montague-Capulet opposition to the love of Romeo and Juliet in Shakespeare's play.

Recommended recording: Original cast recording on Columbia SBO 2633, conducted by Franz Allers.

100   Sondheim: *Sweeney Todd*

Libretto by Stephen Sondheim and Hugh Wheeler after a play by Christopher Bond; first performed at the Uris Theatre, New York, in 1978.

Sondheim's score for this so-called musical is warm and melodic, and the work is a superb piece of music theatre, or twentieth-century opera.

Recommended recording: Original cast recording on RCA BLO 3379(2).

an
operatic
glossary

Antefatto   An Italian word meaning 'antecedent fact', and the term used to explain briefly to the audience any background facts or previous events essential to their understanding of the opera, usually through a printed synopsis in the libretto or programme, but sometimes in narration at the beginning of the opera. See also **Argomento.**

Argomento   An Italian word meaning 'argument', an 'argomento' is a summary of the plot or of events considered to have taken place before the beginning of the story, printed by way of preface to the libretto.

Aria   The general term for an extended solo in opera, as opposed to the simpler, non-operatic 'song' or 'Lied'. The diminutive form of the word, 'arietta', refers to the shorter, less complex solo which is usually lighter in character.

Azione sacra   Italian for 'sacred action', this term is used to describe a sacred opera, or an opera on a religious subject.

**Azione
teatrale**

Italian for 'theatrical action', a term used in the seventeenth century to describe a play or an opera.

Ballad opera

A type of opera or musical play which flourished in England in the eighteenth and nineteenth centuries in which the musical numbers, usually in the style of folk songs or simple choruses, were separated by spoken dialogue. *The Beggar's Opera* (q.v.) is an early example, and such popular nineteenth-century works as Balfe's *The Bohemian Girl* and Wallace's *Maritana* are sophisticated descendants of the earlier *ballad opera,* as are the Gilbert and Sullivan operettas, or Savoy Operas (q.v.).

Baritone

The word, from the Greek 'baritonos' or 'heavy tone', is used to describe not the heaviest but the middle type of male singing voice, higher in range and lighter in timbre than bass, but lower and heavier than tenor. See **Bass.**

Bass

From the Italian 'basso' (low), the bass is the lowest type of male voice. As with the baritone voice, there are a number of recognised categories; for instance *basso profondo,* which the Germans call 'Tiefer Bass' (low bass), the kind of voice for which Mozart wrote the role of Sarastro in *The Magic Flute,* and 'basso buffo' or comic bass (Osmin in *Die Entführung aus dem Serail* or Don Basilio in *The Barber of Seville*). 'Bass-baritone' is a term used in German and English to describe a voice whose quality has the lightness of a baritone but whose range lacks the higher baritone notes. The role of Wotan in Wagner's *Ring* is most appropriately sung by such a voice.

Bel canto

The Italian term for 'beautiful singing' has come to be used both to describe a method of singing, favoured by the old Italian teachers, in which smoothness and elegance were aimed for, perhaps at the expense of dramatic expression, and to describe the type of opera written in Italy from the eighteenth century until the emergence of Verdi in the middle of the nineteenth century, in which such vocal qualities were called for. The 'bel canto' operas are understood to mean those of Rossini, Bellini and Donizetti, and their followers.

Bocca chiusa Italian for 'closed mouth', this direction to the singer that the notes are to be hummed is sometimes found in scores, for instance in the Humming Chorus in Puccini's *Madama Butterfly* and in the final act of Verdi's *Rigoletto* where the humming voices represent the howling wind.

Brindisi Italian for a drinking song, of which there are many examples in opera, two of the most famous being the chorus led by Iago in the first act of Verdi's *Otello* and the song sung by Alfredo and Violetta near the beginning of the same composer's *La Traviata.*

Bühnenfest- German for stage festival play, this was Wagner's term to
spiel describe his tetralogy, *The Ring of the Nibelung.* Wagner described his *Parsifal* as a 'Bühnenweihfestspiel' or, literally, 'stage consecration festival play'.

Cabaletta The term has had several meanings, but is now used to describe the final section of an aria, usually in a fast tempo. Sometimes, the cabaletta is virtually an aria in itself, preceded by an aria in slower tempo, from which it is separated by a short declamatory passage. The popular tenor aria, 'Di quella pira', in Verdi's *Il Trovatore* is, in fact, the cabaletta of the tenor's aria, 'Ah si, ben mio'. In the soprano aria, 'Dove sono', from Mozart's *The Marriage of Figaro,* the quick, concluding section which begins with the words 'Ah, se almen la mia costanza' is the aria's cabaletta.

Cadenza The Italian word for 'cadence' has come to mean an elaborate flourish preceding a final cadence. In vocal music, the cadenza is sometimes written into the score, though formerly it would have been left for the singer to improvise. The practice of writing the cadenza into the score has been customary since the time of Rossini, who disapproved of the intrusive embellishments singers tended to insert into his scores.

Cantilena The word used to mean a cradle-song or an old, popular song, but now is used to describe a smoothly flowing melody or the ability to sing a passage smoothly and gracefully.

Cartellone Literally the playbill or placard, the word has come to be used to mean the list of operas to be performed during a given season.

Cavatina Literally the diminutive of 'cavata', an arioso passage 'carved out of' the preceding music, the cavatina is a short, simple aria. Sometimes the term is used to indicate the first part of an aria, which is followed by the cabaletta.

Chest voice A term used in the teaching of singing: the chest voice is the lower of the two registers, chest and head. The chest register is used mainly by the male voice, while the head register predominates in the female voice. Female singers, however, use the chest register to achieve power in the projection of their lower notes.

Claque A group of supporters, found mainly in Italian opera houses, who hire themselves to singers and provide applause in return for payment. In the nineteenth century, the claque was powerful in a number of opera houses in France, Germany and Austria as well as in Italy.

Colla voce 'With the voice': a direction to the accompanying instrument or instruments to follow the exact tempo and phrasing of the voice part.

Coloratura Literally 'coloration' or 'colouring', the term as used in music refers to brilliantly ornamented writing for the voice, or, by extension, the type of voice agile enough to specialise in such music.

Comic opera An expression sometimes used in English either as a translation of the French *opéra comique* or the Italian *opera buffa,* or as a description of the Gilbert and Sullivan operettas.

Commedia per musica A term used in Italy in the eighteenth and early nineteenth centuries to describe any comic opera.

Comprimario Literally 'with the principal', the word is now used to describe the secondary singer, or one who supports the principal singers. Roles in opera are either principal or comprimario roles. A so-called 'principal' role can be quite small, but will be described as such if it contains a solo number. The comprimario will rarely have even one short solo, but will be heard in recitative or in ensembles. Inez and Ruiz in *Il Trovatore*, Spoletta in *Tosca*, are comprimario roles. Goro in *Madame Butterfly* is a comprimario role, but Suzuki is a principal role.

Contralto The lowest category of female voice, the others being mezzo-soprano and soprano. Nowadays, a number of voices which would formerly have been trained as contraltos are classified as mezzo-sopranos and encouraged to extend their range upwards. The old deep contralto voice, the voice of Clara Butt or Ernestine Schumann-Heink, is disappearing.

Counter-tenor A male tenor voice which relies to a very large extent on the use of the head register, of falsetto (q.v.). Popular in church music of mediaeval and classical times, this type of voice makes its appearance in modern opera in the role of Oberon in Britten's *A Midsummer Night's Dream*.

Couplets This French term, which originally meant 'stanzas', came to be used for any strophic song in opera, i.e. a song containing a number of stanzas sung to the same music.

Dramaturg The member of the staff of German opera houses who is responsible for the dramatic or literary aspects of the operas to be performed. He may undertake research, or translate libretti, and will usually edit the theatre programme as well. His functions in English and American opera houses are often undertaken by the press or public relations officer.

Dramma giocoso   A 'jocose drama' in the eighteenth century was a serious opera with comic episodes or *vice versa*, e.g. Mozart's *Don Giovanni*.

Dramma per musica   A 'drama through music' in the eighteenth century was either a libretto or drama intended to be set to music or the ensuing opera itself.

Durch-komponiert   This German word, 'through-composed', when applied to an opera, indicates an opera which is composed throughout, in the sense that there is no dialogue or recitative but only continuous music.

Elenco artistico   Literally the 'artistic list', the 'elenco artistico' is the list of the names of artists engaged by an opera company to appear during the season.

Entr'acte   A piece of music performed between the acts of an opera, by way of prelude to the next act, or sometimes played between scenes, perhaps to cover the time taken by a scene change.

Falsetto   The false or artificial method of producing the voice employed by male singers either to imitate the female voice or to produce high notes with a soft, crooning sound. It is also the method of voice production used by counter-tenors.

Fioritura   In vocal terms, a decoration of the actual melody, or what is also nowadays referred to as 'coloratura' (q.v.).

Grand opera   Often used to refer to opera which contains no spoken dialogue, the term is more properly used as a translation of the French 'grand opéra', an epic work in four or five acts with ballet, characteristic of the Paris Opera in the first half of the nineteenth century. Meyerbeer was a leading composer of grand opera.

Heldentenor   The German term for 'heroic tenor' or dramatic tenor voice. Most of the tenor roles in the operas of Wagner (e.g. Siegfried and Siegmund in *The Ring,* Lohengrin, Tannhäuser) are written for this type of voice, more forceful than the lyric tenor and usually more baritonal in timbre.

In alt

The term used to describe the musical notes in the octave immediately above the treble stave. The octave above that is *in altissimo.*

Ingénue

The French adjective for 'artless' is used in its feminine form to describe the younger female roles in comic opera, usually written for light soprano voices.

Intermezzo

The Italian word for 'interlude' is used to describe an orchestral interlude between the scenes of an opera, but was used in the seventeenth and eighteenth centuries to describe short, self-contained musical pieces which were inserted between the acts of plays.

Lamento

A tragic aria in classical Italian opera, usually sung by the hero immediately before the dénouement. Two famous examples are 'Lasciatemi morire' from Monteverdi's *Arianna* and 'Che faro senza Euridice?' from Gluck's *Orpheus and Eurydice.*

Leitmotif

The German term for 'leading motif', widely used by Wagner to describe his method of using musical themes or phrases to identify not only individual characters but states of mind, emotions and subconscious feelings.

Libretto

Literally 'little book', a libretto is the dramatic script of an opera or operetta, the words provided by the poet or dramatist to be set by the composer.

Lied

The German word for 'song' has come to mean a particular kind of German song. At first written for performance in the home by Mozart, Beethoven, Schubert, Schumann, the *Lied* was self-consciously developed into 'art song' by Brahms and, especially, Wolf. The term is used in German opera to indicate a solo song rather simpler in structure than an aria.

Maestro	Italian for 'master', the term is used in Italy when addressing a composer or conductor, and its use has spread abroad, to the extent that British and American musicians will often address their conductor, whether or not he is Italian, as 'Maestro'.
Masque	One of the forerunners of opera, the masque is a sixteenth-century entertainment combining the arts of poetry, music, dancing and elaborate architectural design.
Melodrama	A composition in which words are recited against a musical background; the device is occasionally used in opera for dramatic effect, as, for instance, in Act II of Beethoven's *Fidelio* where Leonore and Rocco speak their dialogue above the orchestral comment.
Messa di voce	A vocal effect: the art of swelling and then diminishing the tone on a sustained single note, much favoured by singers of the *bel canto* era.
Mezza voce	The Italian term for 'half voice' is used as a direction to the singer to sing with moderate force, between extremes of soft and loud.
Mezzo-soprano	The middle category of female voice, between contralto and soprano, the mezzo-soprano appears to be replacing the contralto.
Music drama	The term used to describe operas in which the dramatic content is thought to be especially important, or in which musical and dramatic elements are so unified that the drama comes to take precedence. The mature operas of Wagner are so described, though in fact *Don Giovanni* (Mozart) is no less a music drama than *Tristan und Isolde*.
Music theatre	A modern, usually small-scale, offshoot of 'music drama', indicating an attempt by certain contemporary composers to produce opera without the trappings of nineteenth-century operatic extravagance. Music theatre pieces are written for small casts and accompanied by instrumental ensembles with far fewer players than in the conventional opera orchestras.

149

Number opera	An opera, such as those written in the eighteenth and earlier part of the nineteenth centuries, written in separate 'numbers', i.e. with self-contained arias, duets, ensembles, separated by recitative. These were numbered in the printed score, for convenience.
Obbligato	Italian for 'obligatory', the word has come to mean, in vocal music, a solo instrumental part used to provide support for the voice.
Opera-ballet	When opera was introduced into France, ballet played a more important role than in other countries, and the earliest operas were hybrid entertainments known as opera-ballets. A well-known example is Rameau's *Les Indes galantes.*
Opera buffa	The Italian term for comic opera.
Opéra comique	Literally 'comic opera', the term came to be used to describe the type of French opera which, unlike grand opera, made use of spoken dialogue between musical numbers. Bizet's *Carmen* is an *opéra comique,* though it is by no means a comic opera.
Opera seria	'Serious opera' or seventeenth- and eighteenth-century serious opera, usually on classical subjects. The operas of Gluck are examples of *opera seria.* By the time of Mozart, the genre was undergoing a number of changes, and Mozart's more humanized music dramas helped to hasten its decline. Mozart, however, composed one of the greatest examples of *opera seria* in *Idomeneo.*
Operetta	'Little opera' (or 'opérette' in French) used to mean precisely that, a short opera, but came in the nineteenth century to mean the lighter type of opera, usually with spoken dialogue separating the musical numbers, and with comic or sentimental plots. Offenbach's *La vie parisienne* is a typical example of French operetta, while Léhar's *The Merry Widow* and Johann Strauss's *Die Fledermaus* are the most famous Viennese operettas.

Overture   An instrumental prelude to an opera. The early operas usually
began without an overture, but the eighteenth-century operas
mostly had separate, formal overtures, a practice which
continued until the mature works of Verdi and Wagner. Some
overtures utilized thematic material from the opera; others did
not. Since the last operas of Verdi, the overture has become
the rare exception, rather than the rule.

Parlando   Literally 'speaking', a direction to allow the singing voice, in a
passage of recitative or arioso, to be produced as it would be
in speech, rather than to sustain the tone as in singing.

Patter song   A comic song in a very fast tempo, in which the words are
sung as quickly as possible, the tune often being an unmemorable marking of the poetic rhythm. There are a number
of examples in the Savoy operas of Gilbert and Sullivan.

Portamento   Literally 'carrying', the ability to carry the voice smoothly from
one note to the next, an effect sometimes exaggerated when
the singer anticipates the next note by sliding onto it.

Posse   This German word for 'buffoonery' or 'tomfoolery' is used to
describe the kind of musical farce which emerged in Vienna
in the late eighteenth century, and reached its heights in the
nineteenth century in the plays of Raimund and Nestroy, with
music by such theatre composers as Drechsler and Wenzel
Müller.

Prelude   An orchestral piece played before the curtain rises on the
opera, the Prelude differs from the Overture usually by being
shorter and less complex in structure.

Prima donna   'First lady', or the leading female singer in an opera or an
opera company. Precedence is given to the soprano over the
mezzo-soprano voice. Similarly the 'primo uomo' or leading
man is more likely to be tenor than baritone or bass.

Prompter	In Italian opera houses the prompter, concealed in a box-like compartment downstage centre, functions not only when a performer suffers a lapse of memory as in a spoken play but throughout the performance by anticipating and uttering the singer's next entry, presumably on the ground that prevention is better than cure. Italian singers tend to rely on the prompter, while German- and English-speaking singers do not.
Recitative	A style of writing for the voice in which the rhythms and inflections of speech are retained. In opera, it is used for scenes of dialogue, as opposed to the more reflective lyrical scenes in which the characters express their feelings through arias, duets or ensembles.
Repetiteur	Literally 'rehearser', the member of the opera house's musical staff who is responsible for coaching the singers in their roles.
Romanza	A song of tender character, usually simpler than an aria, and devoid of any element of vocal display.
Savoy Operas	The name given to the operettas of Gilbert and Sullivan, many of which were first produced at the Savoy Theatre, London.
Scena	A solo scene in opera, often consisting of an extended recitative and aria with cabaletta.
Scenario	An outline of the libretto or synopsis of the plot of an opera.
Singspiel	German term for a play with songs, which has come to be used to describe the German equivalent of 'opéra comique': an opera in German whose musical numbers are separated by spoken dialogue. A popular example is Mozart's *Abduction from the Harem. The Magic Flute* is formally a Singspiel, though rarely thought of as such.
Sitzprobe	Literally 'sitting rehearsal', this is the term used for the first complete rehearsal of an opera with orchestra, the soloists and chorus seated on stage and rehearsing musically, without stage movement.

Soprano   The highest category of female singing voice, which is sub-divided into dramatic, lyric, and light (or soubrette, leggiera) soprano.

Sotto voce   Italian phrase, directing the singer to sing softly, as an aside.

Soubrette   The term used to describe such lyric soprano roles as Susanna in *The Marriage of Figaro,* or Adele in *Die Fledermaus:* the pert, cheeky, light comedienne role, as often as not a serving-girl.

Spieloper   German term for 'acting opera' or an opera in which dramatic talent is especially important, usually because of a preponderance of spoken dialogue. In other words, a *Singspiel* or *opéra comique.*

Spieltenor   'Acting tenor', or a tenor who is primarily an actor, often specialising in comedy roles requiring adept handling of dialogue in light opera or operetta. In *Die Fledermaus,* the role of Eisenstein is suitable for a 'Spieltenor', while the other tenor role of Alfred calls for a strong lyric tenor.

Spinto   Literally 'pushed', the term is used to describe the type of voice which is more forceful than the lyric tenor but not necessarily as heavy as the dramatic tenor. Most of Verdi's middle-period tenor roles are written for such a voice.

Sprechgesang   Literally 'speech-song', the term is used to describe a form of musical declamation when the voice changes its pitch from note to note as in singing, but does not sustain its tone, allowing it to be produced as in speech. The notes then seem to be spoken rather than sung.

Stagione   Italian for 'season', the *Stagione* in an operatic context means the opera season. It has also come to be used to describe the system of casting operas separately with different singers throughout a season, as opposed to the repertory system in which a permanant ensemble performs a large number of operas in repertory.

Stretta   Literally 'tightening', the *stretta* is the passage in an accelerated tempo which brings the aria, duet or ensemble to an exciting conclusion.

Tenor   The highest category of male singing voice, usually subdivided into dramatic tenor (or *Heldentenor* in the German repertory), lyric tenor, tenore spinto, and tenore di grazia. Examples of the heroic or dramatic tenor roles are Siegfried in *The Ring* or Otello in Verdi's opera; lyric tenor – Alfredo in *La Traviata*; spinto – Riccardo in *Un Ballo in maschera*; tenore di grazia – Nemorino in *L'Elisir d'amore*.

Tenuto   Italian for 'held'; a direction to the singer to sustain a note for its full value.

Tessitura   Italian for 'texture', but used to describe the average vocal range of a piece of music or a complete operatic role. Though it may contain one or two isolated high notes, the music for a particular role may in general be written around the middle of the singer's range, in which case the role will be said to be of medium tessitura. The role of the Queen of Night in Mozart's *The Magic Flute* has a high tessitura.

Transposition   To re-write or to perform a piece of music, e.g. an aria, in a key higher or lower than that in which it was composed is to transpose it. Opera singers often transpose arias downwards (or, less frequently, upwards) when they can no longer reach the extreme notes in the original keys.

Travesti   Past participle of the French verb 'travestir', meaning 'to disguise', the term is used to describe male roles (usually adolescents) written by composers to be performed by females. Examples include Cherubino in *The Marriage of Figaro*, Octavian in *Der Rosenkavalier* and Orlovsky in *Die Fledermaus* (though Orlovsky is sometimes performed by a tenor).

Treble   A child's voice singing in the soprano range is described as a treble. Miles and Flora in Benjamin Britten's *The Turn of the Screw* are examples of operatic treble roles.

Verismo Italian for 'realism', the term describes the school of Italian opera which flourished briefly in the late nineteenth and early twentieth centuries, whose subjects and music were at the time thought to be more realistic than those of earlier opera. A kind of forerunner to the British 'kitchen sink' school of drama in the mid-twentieth century. Mascagni and Leoncavallo with *Cavalleria Rusticana* and *Pagliacci* were early exponents of 'verismo', and some of the operas of Puccini can also be said to belong to the genre.

Vibrato Italian for 'vibrated'. The human singing voice naturally vibrates, or fluctuates in pitch and intensity. The well-trained singer whose voice is in good condition is able to control his vibrato. An uncontrolled vibrato sounds like, and is unkindly referred to as, a wobble.

Zarzuela Spanish equivalent of operetta, the Zarzuela takes its name from the palace near Madrid where this type of entertainment came into existence in the seventeenth century.

suggestions for further reading

general

Brockway, Wallace and Weinstock, Herbert:
The World of Opera. Methuen

Cooper, Martin: *Opéra-Comique.* Max Parrish

Cooper, Martin: *Russian Opera.* Max Parrish

Crosten, William I.: *French Grand Opera.* Da Capo

Dent, Edward J.: *Opera.* Penguin (rev. ed. 1949)

Hope-Wallace, Philip: *A Picture-history of Opera.* The Hulton Press

Kerman, Joseph: *Opera as Drama.* Alfred Knopf, New York, 1956

Kobbé's Complete Opera Book:
edited and revised by the Earl of Harewood. Putnam

Newman, Ernest: *Opera Nights.* Putnam

Newman, Ernest: *More Opera Nights.* Putnam

Opera: monthly magazine, edited by Harold Rosenthal

Rosenthal, Harold and Warrack, John: *Concise Oxford
    Dictionary of Opera.* OUP (rev. 1978)

Swanston, Hamish F. G.: *In Defence of Opera.* Penguin

Weaver, William: *The Golden Century of Italian Opera.*
    Thames & Hudson

books on individual composers

Bellini
Herbert Weinstock: Vincenzo Bellini. Weidenfeld & Nicolson

Britten
Eric Walter White: *Benjamin Britten, His Life and Operas.*
    Faber (rev. 1970)

Donizetti
Herbert Weinstock: *Donizetti.* Methuen

Mozart
Charles Osborne: *The Complete Operas of Mozart.* Gollancz
Spike Hughes: *Famous Mozart Operas.* Dover
Brophy, Brigid: *Mozart the Dramatist.* Faber

Puccini
Mosco Carner: *Puccini.* Duckworth (rev. 1974)

Rossini
Herbert Weinstock: *Rossini.* Oxford

Richard Strauss
William Mann: *Richard Strauss, a Critical Study of the Operas.*
    Cassell

Verdi
Charles Osborne: *The Complete Operas of Verdi.* Gollancz
Spike Hughes: *Famous Verdi Operas.* Robert Hale

Wagner
Gutman, Robert W.: *Richard Wagner.* Penguin
Ernest Newman: *Wagner Nights.* Putnam
Charles Osborne: *Wagner and his World.* Thames & Hudson

index